A HANDBOOK ON QUANTITY FOOD MANAGEMENT

by

E. EVELYN SMITH
Associate Professor
of
Institution Management
University of Illinois
Urbana, Illinois

Third Printing 1957

BURGESS PUBLISHING CO.
Minneapolis 15 - Minnesota

ACKNOWLEDGEMENTS

The writer expresses her thanks to various members of the Institution Management staff of the University of Illinois, especially to Jean Vertovec. Thanks is also extended to Mrs. Pearl Janssen for her critical review of several chapters and to Miss Agnes Doster for her help in editing the manuscript.

PREFACE

This handbook is designed primarily for classes in Institution Management and Quantity Cookery. The material should be helpful to managers of restaurants and school lunchrooms and to other operators who are striving to serve quality food.

The topics deal with the tools and controls of Quantity Cookery Management based upon the scientific, technological, economic, social and aesthetic values. Major emphasis is placed on the use of these tools and controls in the actual operations involved in the management, preparation and serving of foods to groups.

Some aspects of management will need more intensive study than can be included in this handbook. These will be touched on briefly in order to integrate all aspects of food management. Further study will be possible, by using the suggested bibliography at the end of each chapter. In order to develop in the students, a searching and problem-solving attitude, suggestions for problems and term papers are also included.

A suggested organization and plan for managing a quantity cookery laboratory is included in the appendix. Some additional charts, instructions and studies are also included.

TABLE OF CONTENTS

Pages

3 (Good Meals) + Careful Preparation = Health

Chapter I

INTRODUCTION

It has long been recognized that the culture of a nation can be measured by its food habits and customs. Much of our present day social and economic life centers around the serving of food in the home or in public eating establishments. The fact that there is an increasing tendency for people to "dine-out" affords managers of food service establishments the opportunity as well as the responsibility to advance the health, welfare, culture and happiness of the nation by serving food of high quality.

Quality food is food that has retained as many of its natural properties as possible. It should be appealing to the eye, should be palatable and should have nutritive value. Eye appeal depends on the skillful use of color, form and texture, arrangement, quantity and garnish. Palatability is determined by odor, temperature, flavor, texture, and consistency. In short, quality food must be food that is good to <u>look at</u>, <u>tastes good</u>, <u>is good for you</u> and <u>is safe</u>.

Quality in food cannot be achieved by careless or haphazard methods. To the long established art of cookery must be added methods and controls that have been developed by scientific investigations, engineering and technological accomplishments and tried business procedures. It is only through the constant and intelligent use of these known controls that quality food can consistently be produced in quantity with the least expenditure of time, effort, and material. The scientific approach to quantity cookery involves specific definition of the problems, the understanding and intelligent use of the scientific principles involved and the rigid control of all conditions.

Wisely selected food, scientifically prepared and served will be quality food whether in large or small quantity. The principles are the same, but there is more danger of undesirable changes in quantity cookery due to the complexity of the problem and the different techniques required.

PROBLEMS PECULIAR TO QUANTITY FOOD MANAGEMENT

1. Adjustment of cooking, timing, and method to allow heat penetration to greater masses.
2. Use of machines and large equipment for long and heavy processes.
3. Use of steam and steam equipment as fuel.
4. Distribution and serving of food.
5. Personnel.

1. <u>Adjustment of Time and Method</u>: Food cooked in too large amounts or cooked too long will lose much of its quality and nutritive value. In order to prevent this, it is necessary to have a short and direct flow from production to service. This can best be accomplished by cutting to a minimun the post-preparation and post-stove time and by cooking food in relays

at well-timed intervals during the serving period. The use of equipment of appropriate construction and size is also an important factor.

2. Use of Machines and Large Equipment: In order to decrease the time and labor involved in the long and heavy processes of quantity work, the modern kitchen employs as much power driven equipment and as many labor-saving devices as possible.

3. Use of Steam and Steam Equipment: The use of high pressure steam and steam equipment is particularily suited to quantity cookery. It is cheap and clean. It cuts down the cooking time and preserves quality and nutritive value and makes staggered cookery possible.

4. Distribution and Serving: In quantity food service, there may be a wide difference between the quality of food as purchased and prepared and its quality when actually served. In this respect, quantity food production differs most from small quantity. To maintain quality it is necessary to reduce to a minimum the time between final preparation and serving.

5. Personnel: In the large kitchen the personnel problems are multiplied by the number of employees. Workers in the food industry may be highly specialized and technically trained or they may be entirely unskilled. The problem of selection, training and supervising these workers in their many activities presents a distinct challenge to management.

TOOLS AND CONTROLS OF MANAGEMENT

The previous presentation of some of the complex problems of quantity food management and of the responsibilities of the manager in meeting them would indicate that the tools and controls are many and diverse. They embrace the scientific, technological, economic and aesthetic aspects of management. Managers and students should become increasingly aware of these aspects and of their application to the problems and techniques of quantity food management.

The various tools and controls of quantity food management will be discussed in succeeding chapters under the following headings which indicate the organization of the handbook material.

INTRODUCTION

ORGANIZATION AND PLANNING: Menu Making, Buying, Scheduling

CONTROLLED PREPARATION PRECEDURES AS APPLIED TO QUANTITY COOKERY

MODERN AND MECHANIZED FOOD UNITS

STANDARDIZATION: Methods, Recipes and Portions

WORK SIMPLIFICATION TECHNIQUES: The Use of Proper Practices, Motions, Equipment and Machinery

CONSERVATION AND WASTE CONTROL: Keeping Within the Budget

SANITATION AND ACCIDENT PREVENTION

MERCHANDIZING AND SALESMANSHIP: Food Attractively and Artistically Displayed

SERVICE OF FOOD: Suitable and Efficient to Groups of Various Sizes and Under Varying Conditions

PERSONNEL

Chapter II

ORGANIZATION AND PLANNING

Organization means "bringing into effective correlation all the parts of a whole, each part having a function peculiar to itself, yet having a definite relationship to the whole". As the group becomes larger, there is more necessity for a definite and concrete organization.

The manager's responsibility is to have a pattern and plan for all operations so that they may go forward with the least expenditure of time, effort, material and money to make it possible to see and at the same time to direct the overall organization. This chapter will deal with three aspects of organization and planning.

A. Menus
B. Buying Practices
C. Work Schedules and Instruction

A. MENUS THAT ARE SUITABLE, WORKABLE AND WELL PLANNED

In order to have well planned menus it is necessary to have a well worked out menu pattern which is suitable to the clientele and workable as related to the staff and equipment available. A menu should not have too many operations or emphasis on the wrong foods. It should always be planned to meet the nutritional needs of the group to be fed.

Factors Involved in Menu Making

1. Clientele
   a. Racial habits
   b. Likes and dislikes
   c. Nutritional needs
   d. Economic status

2. Markets
   a. Economic trends
   b. Grades, quality, and cost of foods available from competing firms
   c. Time of delivery
   d. Amount of purchase, to prevent emergency buying or spoilage
   e. Availability, cost, and quality of foods at different seasons

3. Food Budget
   a. Money available for food
   b. Cost of raw food
   c. Proper ratio between high and low cost dishes

4. Preparation in Relation to Employees
   a. Avoid too many last minute processes. There should be a proper ratio between foods that can be prepared early without deterioration and those requiring last minute preparation.
   b. Avoid too many long jobs, especially for one cook.
   c. Avoid too complicated processes or emphasis on wrong kinds of food for available employees. Plan meals the staff can do well.
   d. Have records on timing and yields.
   e. Allow time for portioning and garnishing.

5. Equipment, Work Space
   a. Menus should conform to limitations of equipment and physical facilities.

6. Distribution and Service
   a. Menus will need to be planned in relation to the type of service and the distance over which food must be transported for service. Direct routing and cooperation of all concerned will prevent undue holding.

7. Salesmanship and Merchandising of Food

8. Other Food Sources
   a. Surplus commodities
   b. Donations
   c. Federal aid

9. Types of Groups to be Served
   a. If many groups or types of meals must be served from a central kitchen, a master menu with modifications should be used.

      Example:
      A hospital where nurses, doctors, and patients are served.

Well Planned Menu Making Techniques

1. Plan a regular uninterrupted time for making your menus when you are not too fatigued. Choose a quiet place.

2. Have available all records, charts and books which will be helpful.

3. Have a well organized, classified and usable menu chart. This will be a guide to menu making and will, if kept up to date, suggest ideas and help to prevent monotony and repetition in menu making. Ideas for menu charts can be collected from books, magazines, visits to restaurants and many other sources.

4. Formulate a workable menu pattern. This menu pattern should be planned to meet the needs of the various groups of individuals served, and should be based on definite information as discussed above.

   Examples:
   a. Residence hall menu with no choices
   b. School lunch with limited choice
   c. Commercial cafeteria, restaurant or hospital with varied and selective menus.

5. Make menus for one week in advance, when possible. Use menu chart and other sources to get interest, variety and nutritional adequacy and to avoid repetition. Recheck menus daily to use up left-overs and to meet other problems. Do not leave these daily adjustments to the cook's judgment.

Some Guides to Menu Making

1. Consider your patrons as to age, sex, race, occupation, and nutritional needs.

2. Consider season, holidays and fast days.

3. Consider cost and selling price. Be sure to serve what patrons want and sell at a price they can pay.

4. Plan the menu so that the patron secures a balanced meal and one which will meet the nutritional standards for a normal diet.

5. Offer choices so that a patron may choose well balanced meals of the type desired.

   Example:
   a. A light luncheon
   b. A light dinner
   c. A heavy dinner

6. Plan for variety in menus.
   a. Have variety from day to day rather than too many choices at one meal.
   b. Have variety in distinct types, such as vegetables and fruit salads.
   c. Never serve the same dish on the same day two or more consecutive weeks.
   d. Do not repeat any dish oftener than at eight or ten day intervals.

7. Avoid having all popular dishes in one meal and all uninteresting dishes another meal.

8. Avoid a run of foods of the same type or shape.

9. Serve foods in season.

10. Vary form in which foods are served and cooked, especially in spring. Use new recipes.

11. Use left-overs in a variety of different ways.

12. Give interesting and descriptive names to foods.

13. Style food by skillful garnish, use of color, and by interesting serving dishes.

14. Serve foods in standard portions and serve in appropriate sized dishes.

15. Be guided by popularity studies and study of plate returns.

MENU CHART

In making menus, effort should be made to have both variety and contrast in type of menu items. It is suggested that students or managers establish a classified menu chart, listing varieties of dishes and ways of preparing them. This will be a great time saver in making varied, interesting, suitable and workable menus. The following pages suggest a form for such charts which could be filled in by students or managers.

SOUPS

Stock	Cream	Chowders	Others	Soup Accomp.
Scotch Broth	Tomato	Corn	Oyster Bisque	Melba Toast

MEATS

High Cost	Medium Cost	Low Cost	Meat Sauce
Swiss Steak	Beef Stew	Cream Chipped Beef	Barbeque

FISH

High Cost	Medium Cost - Extended	Low Cost	Fish Sauces
Halibut Steak	Salmon Loaf	Codfish Balls	Tartar

MEAT SUBSTITUTES AND ENTREES

Egg Dishes	Cheese Dishes	Legumes	Starchy	Vegetable
Marigold Eggs	Cheese Fondue	Boston Baked Beans	Macaroni and Cheese	Spinach au gratin

VEGETABLES				
POTATOES		OTHER VEGETABLES		
White	Sweet Potatoes	Asparagus Creamed Beans Buttered Beets Harvard Carrots Glazed		
Mashed	Glazed			

SALADS

Main Course	Veg. and Relish	Fruit	Gelatin		Salad Dressing
			Vegetable	Fruit	
Tuna Fish	Cole Slaw	Waldorf	Perfection	Pear and Lime	Boiled

DESSERTS

Cake Type Dessert	Puddings	Gelatin and Fruit	Sauces
Gingerbread	Custards	Snow Pudding	Lemon

CAKES		PIES		
Cake	Frostings	One Crust	Two Crust	Chiffon
Chocolate	Mocha	Butterscotch	Cherry	Lemon

HOT BREADS

Biscuits	Muffins and Quick Breads	Rolls and Yeast Breads
Plain	Bran	Cloverleaf

B. GOOD BUYING PRACTICES

In this manual it is not possible to deal with the specifics of purchasing. A few general guides are suggested to show the integration of the problems.

1. Have a buying Schedule
    a. Plan a regular schedule for daily, weekly, monthly and yearly buying based on anticipated needs and foods on hand.
    b. Plan menus and make market order concurrently.
    c. Avoid a rigid buying schedule and standing orders which will limit menus.
    d. Eliminate emergency buying by use of your planned buying schedule.

2. Utilize foods that are on hand, in season and readily available.

3. Follow general buying system of institution.

4. Use printed forms, when possible.

5. Buy by specification as to size, grade and form.

6. Decide a proper quantity to purchase by using quantity and yield tables. Buy in wholesale units.

7. Avoid too heavy inventories.

8. Make requisitions or market orders that are concise, well organized and specific, as to amount, size, quality and wholesale unit.

9. Check goods received as to quantity and quality.

10. Record total cost and file sales slips.

For further study of purchasing, see suggested forms and bibliography.

1. SAMPLE PURCHASE FORM

DATE					
ITEMS	AMOUNT	SPECIFICATION	Price VENDER	Quotation VENDER	CHECKED

2. SAMPLE STOREROOM WITHDRAWAL SLIP

Number or Amount	Unit or Size	Item	Brand	Checked		
				Storeroom Man	Manager	Entered on Inventory Card

C. CAREFULLY PLANNED WORK SCHEDULE

The work of each unit should be specifically planned. The purpose is not merely to get tasks done, but to get them done in the best way and in the shortest time with the least effort and at the same time to retain maximum nutritive value and quality food.

A work sheet should be planned for each worker. This is really a job analysis, showing what is to be done, who is to do it, when and how it is to be done.

Procedure for Making a Work Sheet:

1. List all jobs to be done, in sequence, and divide them into the various work units.

2. Assign each job to one person, who should be entirely responsible for completing it. A worker may help others if necessary, but if the plan is carefully worked out, this is not necessary.

3. Avoid cross-organization. Organize kitchen work in units. A standard plan comprises range, salad, pastry units. Each worker should be assigned to a specific unit and should not be expected to work in different units and on dissimilar jobs.

4. Dovetail all operations when possible.

5. Plan a time schedule and job assignments which the worker can be expected to complete on time.

6. State specifically in each work schedule the amount of food to be prepared, the exact recipe to be used, the size of servings and any other necessary instructions.

SAMPLE FORMS FOR WORK SHEETS

Date	Range Unit			
Menu Item	Amount to Prepare	Amount Left over	Prepared by	Special Directions
Soups				
Entrees				
Vegetables				

Date	Salad Unit			
Menu Item	Amount to Prepare	Amount Left over	Prepared by	Special Directions
Salads				
Salad dressings				

	Bake Shop			
Menu Item	Amount to Prepare	Amount Left over	Prepared by	Special Directions
Desserts				
Cake				
Pie				
Hot Bread				
Fruit				

SAMPLE FORMS FOR WORK SHEETS

Date	Range Unit			
Menu Item	Amount to Prepare	Amount Left over	Prepared by	Special Directions
Soups				
Entrees				
Vegetables				

Date	Salad Unit			
Menu Item	Amount to Prepare	Amount Left over	Prepared by	Special Directions
Salads				
Salad dressings				

	Bake Shop			
Menu Item	Amount to Prepare	Amount Left over	Prepared by	Special Directions
Desserts				
Cake				
Pie				
Hot Bread				
Fruit				

DAILY FOOD CONSUMPTION SHEET

Date ______________________ Total served ______________

Weather ____________________ Students _________________

Cost	Selling price	Size portion	Menu item	Prepared	Sold	Left Over	Remarks
			Soup				
			Entrees				
			Vegetables				
			Salads				
			Hot bread				
			Desserts				
			Fruit				

DAILY FOOD CONSUMPTION SHEET

Date ______________________ Total served ______________

Weather ______________________ Students ______________

Cost	Selling price	Size portion	Menu item	Prepared	Sold	Left Over	Remarks
			Soup				
			Entrees				
			Vegetables				
			Salads				
			Hot bread				
			Desserts				
			Fruit				

SUGGESTED STUDIES ON ORGANIZATION AND PLANNING

Menus

1. Suggest and outline studies that will give information on patrons.
2. Make a menu pattern for your unit.
3. Make a menu chart for your unit.
4. Make a week's menu for your unit.
5. Make menus for special occasions and using your quantity tables estimate the amount of each item of food to purchase.
6. Outline short studies to illustrate "styling of the menu".
7. Plan a menu showing a good ratio between high and low cost dishes.
8. Suggest other studies.

Purchasing

1. Outline types of records that will give information on market and market prices.
2. Make graphs of various foods showing seasonal variation.
3. List factors of management and facilities that will determine the amount of foods to be purchased at a time.
4. Collect source material that will help in making out quantity tables.
5. Make a buying schedule that will dovetail with menu-making and that is based on the above listed factors (what, when, where, and how much.)
6. Suggest other studies.

Work Schedules

1. Make out complete work sheets for the preparation of a meal, serving 200 people, using four workers.

BIBLIOGRAPHY ON ORGANIZATION AND PLANNING

Menus

Bryan, Mary de Garmo. School Cafeteria. New York: F. S. Crofts and Company.

Fowler, Sina Faye and Bessie Brooks West. Food for Fifty. New York: John Wiley and Sons.

West, Bessie Brooks and Le Velle Wood. Food Service in Institutions. New York: John Wiley and Sons.

Dodge, Quindara Oliver. Menu Planning and Food Cost Control. Journal of the American Dietetic Association, Vol. 16, pp. 882-890, November, 1940.

Dorcus, Roy M. Food Habits: Their Origin and Control. Journal of the American Dietetic Association, Vol. 18, pp. 738-740, November, 1940.

Selling, Lowell S. Some Psychological Aspects of Nutrition. Journal of the American Dietetic Association, Vol. 18, pp. 741-744, November, 1942.

Carol, Ruth E. Study of Food Selection at the Western Union Cafeteria, New York. Journal of the American Dietetic Association, Vol. 22, pp. 408-410, May, 1946.

Easton, Alice. Five Factors that Affect the Appetite Appeal of Food. Restaurant Management, Vol. LXII, pp. 40, June, 1948.

Gillam, Margaret. The Master Menu. Hospitals, Vol. 23, pp. 77. February, 1949.

Schmid, Fred. Careful Planning Pays. Journal of the American Dietetic Association, Vol. 26, pp. 102-104, February, 1950.

Purchasing

Dahl, J. O. Quantity Food Handbook. Stamford, Conn.: Gold Book Library.

Frooman, A. A. Five Steps in Purchasing. Chicago: Frooman Publishing Company.

Wood, Adeline. Quantity Buying Guides. New York: Ahrens Publishing Company. Vol. I and II.

Chapter III

CONTROLLED PREPARATION PROCEDURES

To develop methods and controls for quantity cookery, it is necessary to understand the scientific and economic principles involved in the processing changes that may take place in the storage, preparation, cooking, distribution and serving of foods in quantity. Many problems and common errors could be avoided or easily corrected if these principles were understood and applied to the techniques in quantity food preparation and service.

In the following discussion, the various processing changes will be reviewed and techniques that will prevent undue losses or undesirable changes in quantity cookery will be indicated.

A summary of the quantity cookery techniques for the preparation and serving of some of the basic foods can be found at the end of the chapter.

PROCESSING CHANGES

A. Nutritive Losses

Experiments have shown that there can be considerable nutritive loss due to improper storage, preparation and cooking and to too long holding after cooking. It has been found that the methods that best preserve the natural qualities of the food will also best preserve the nutritive value. A brief review indicates that vitamin A is stable to heat. The B vitamins are soluble in water and may be destroyed by long cooking. Vitamin C is unstable in heat, air, and soluble in water. Minerals may be lost by improper preparation methods. There may be a considerable loss of other nutrients or a decided change which may affect the rate of digestion. References can be found at the end of the chapter for further study of nutritive losses.

B. Color Losses or Changes

Pigments of foods may be affected by heat, exposure to air and water and by acid-alkaline reactions.

C. Flavor Losses or Changes

Loss of flavor or development of a strong, unpleasant or bitter flavor may result from overcooking, use of improper cooking procedures or too long holding of foods.

D. Texture and Consistency Changes

There may be undesirable changes in texture due to poor recipes, improper cooking techniques or poor timing of production-resulting in long holding.

E. Wilting and Shrinkage

All factors that cause wilting and shrinkage affect both the nutritive value and quality of the food and cause an economic loss. Shrinkage means fewer servings for the money and therefore a higher food cost. The real problem is not how much the food costs, but how much money can be obtained from the sale of it.

F. Temperature Changes

Temperature definitely affects appetite appeal. Foods are more acceptable if served at the correct temperature.

G. Bacteriological Changes

Quality food must be safe food. There is always the potential danger of bacterial growth due to improper handling, storage, cooking and serving. Every precaution must be taken to prevent any contamination of the food.

SCIENTIFIC PRINCIPLES	TECHNIQUES APPLICABLE TO QUANTITY COOKERY
NUTRITIVE LOSSES	PREVENT NUTRITIVE LOSSES
A. Long and improper storage 1. Spoilage of food may be due to poor selection, sorting or storage. 2. Vitamin C may be lost if held at warm temperatures.	A. Store under proper conditions and for short periods. 1. Have a good buying schedule. 2. Buy as near source as possible. 3. Know amounts to buy to avoid long storage periods. 4. Store foods at proper temperatures. 5. Check refrigerators often.
B. Careless Preparation 1. Significant amounts of minerals and vitamins are stored directly under the skin of fruits and vegetables. These are often lost by careless preparation. 2. Outer green leaves are rich in nutritive value. These are often discarded.	B. Prepare Carefully. 1. Use mechanical peelers or train workers to peel correctly. 2. Salvage all valuable parts. 3. Avoid undue trimming of any food. 4. Use vegetable water for soups, gravies and stews. 5. Cook vegetables in natural state when possible. <u>Example</u>: Potatoes with skins on
C. Long Pre-preparation Periods 1. Vitamins and minerals may be lost by long exposure to air and water. 2. The more surface exposed to air and water, the greater the loss of nutrients.	C. Shorten Pre-preparation Periods 1. Prepare foods near time for cooking by use of labor-saving devices and good scheduling. 2. Avoid unnecessary cutting, chopping and shredding. 3. Hold prepared foods by covering with damp cloth and refrigerate at once. 4. Serve foods in natural or raw state when possible.

SCIENTIFIC PRINCIPLES	TECHNIQUES APPLICABLE TO QUANTITY COOKERY
D. Improper Cooking Methods 1. Some vitamins are water soluble and some are destroyed by heat. 2. Minerals are soluble. 3. Enzymes of vegetables need to be inactivated to prevent destruction of vitamins. 4. Proteins may be toughened in cooking, depending on the rate and temperature of coagulation. There may be a loss if cooked rapidly and at too high a temperature. 5. Nutrients may be lost with too much handling of food after cooking. <u>Example</u>: Straining, seiving	D. Use Proper Cooking Methods. 1. Use vegetables of even sizes and maturity to allow quick and even heat penetration. 2. Use steamers or trunnions to cut down on cooking time and to make staggered cookery possible. 3. Avoid overloading of steamer baskets or trunnions. 4. Cook protein foods at low temperatures to avoid shrinkage. Example: Meats roasted at 300-350° F.
E. Long Holding of Food After Cooking 1. Vitamins and minerals and other nutrients may be lost or changed in character upon long standing.	E. Shorten Post-stove and Post-preparation Time. 1. Have a direct flow of all foods from production to service. 2. Use labor-saving devices to assure quick and last minute preparation and prompt and efficient service. 3. Use staggered cookery methods for long service periods. 4. Coordinate production and service by use of good records. <u>Examples</u>: Customer count, popularity studies 5. Avoid long holding on steam tables or heated carts. 6. Avoid re-heating of foods.

F. Holding of Leftovers
   1. Foods held too long, recooked or improperly stored will lose nutrients and volume.
   2. Loss may occur from spoilage.

COLOR LOSSES or CHANGES

A. White Pigments or Flavons
   1. These pigments are fairly stable to heat. Overcooking will cause darkening.
   2. Some foods, especially rice when cooked in alkaline water, may turn a yellow color.
   3. Some fruits contain tannins which will oxidize, causing darkening when exposed to air.

F. Avoid Leftovers
   1. Use charts, yield tables and other data to gauge production.
   2. Use standard recipes and portions to avoid over-production.
   3. Study clientele preferences.
   4. Refrigerate any leftovers promptly and use as soon as possible.

PREVENT COLOR LOSSES

A. White Pigment
   1. Avoid overcooking
      a. Have uniform sizes for quick heat penetration.
      b. Cook short time.
      c. Use staggered cookery for long service periods.
   2. Cream of tartar may be added to alkaline cooking water when cooking rice to prevent discoloration.
   3. Avoid oxidation of fruits.
      a. Prepare fruits that are easily discolored as near serving time as possible.
         Example:
         Apples, bananas
      b. Dip in acid fruit juices to prevent oxidation.

SCIENTIFIC PRINCIPLES	TECHNIQUES APPLICABLE TO QUANTITY COOKERY
B. Red Pigments or Anthocyanins 1. These pigments will turn blue or purplish in color due to exposure to alkali and heat. The color may be restored by the addition of an acid. 2. Red pigments are soluble in water and will fade or lose color.	B. Red Pigments 1. Avoid peeling or exposing large surfaces to water. 2. Cook in weak acid or add acid after cooking. 3. Cook beets in steamer in perforated baskets. 4. Add an acid sauce when holding is necessary.
C. Yellow Pigments or Carotinoids 1. These pigments are not soluble in water and are stable to heat. They are not affected by acids or alkalies. Darkening will result, if overheated, due to the caramelization of the sugars.	C. Yellow Pigments 1. Cut vegetables in uniform sizes for quick and even heat penetration. 2. Cook in steamer in perforated baskets. 3. Avoid overcooking. 4. Hold for short periods on steamtable.
D. Green Pigment or Chlorphyll 1. These pigments are attacked by the volatile and non-volatile acids in the plant which are released during the cooking process, causing an olive green color.	D. Green Pigments 1. Cook in boiling salted water in a trunnion kettle or steamer for short time. 2. Use staggered cookery for long service periods. 3. Use shallow pans on steamtable and replenish often. 4. Hold for short periods on steamtable or in heated carts. 5. Avoid reheating.
E. Other Color Changes 1. Green ring may form around the yolk of hard-cooked eggs due to the reaction of sulphur and iron. 2. Potatoes stored at a low temperature have a high sugar content which causes too rapid and uneven browning and burning.	E. Prevent Color Changes. 1. In hard-cocked eggs: a. Do not overcook. b. Cool quickly. 2. Store potatoes for French fried potatoes at 60-70° F. for some time before using.

FLAVOR LOSSES or CHANGES

A. Flavor Losses
   1. Citrus fruit juices will lose their fresh flavor if juiced and allowed to stand.
   2. Celery and carrots may lose flavor if exposed too long to water or high heat, due to the loss of sugars and minerals which are soluble.
   3. Coffee loses volatile acids upon standing and becomes flat.

B. Flavor Changes
   1. Cabbage, brussel sprouts, kale and turnips contain sinigrin which is easily changed by heat forming hydrogen sulfide which has an unpleasant flavor and odor.
   2. Onions, garlic, leeks contain acids, tannins and volatile substances which give a strong flavor. They are soluble in water and a milder flavor will result if they are cooked in water and if overcooking is prevented.
   3. Fats when overheated decompose and become bitter and irritating due to the formation of acrolin. Fats will break down more quickly if water is present.

PREVENT FLAVOR LOSSES or CHANGES

A. Flavor Losses
   1. Citrus Fruits
      a. Use mechanical or electric juicers to allow last minute preparation.
   2. Celery, carrots
      a. Cook short time.
      b. Avoid long holding.
   3. Do not allow coffee to boil or stand for long period after making.

B. Flavor Changes
   1. Cabbage, brussel sprouts, kale, turnips
      a. Cook in a steamer in water in unperforated baskets or in trunnion kettles.
      b. Cook short time. Use staggered cooking for long service periods.
      c. Hold short time on steamtables.
   2. Onions, garlic, leeks
      a. Select mild onions for cooking.
      b. Cook in steamer in water in unperforated basket or in trunnion kettle.
      c. Avoid overcooking.
      d. Avoid holding on steamtable.
      e. Use staggered cookery for long service periods.
   3. Fats
      a. Select fat with a high smoking point for frying.
      b. Keep fats below smoking point.
      c. Use electric fryers, thermostatically controlled.
      d. Use correct temperature and even heat for frying.

SCIENTIFIC PRINCIPLES

C. Off Flavors
   1. Reheated foods often lose their natural flavor or may develop an off flavor.
   2. Certain baking powders and baking soda, used in excess may cause a bitter residue.
   3. Fats may absorb flavors.

TEXTURE AND CONSISTENCY CHANGES

A. Starch Gels
   1. Foods that are thickened with flour or cornstarch may become thicker and more adhesive upon standing. Additional sugar will increase tenderness of the starch gel, but too much will prevent thickening.
   2. Egg yolks, if not sufficiently cooked after adding to starch mixture will have a thining effect upon standing.
   3. Cooking starch with acids may hydrolize some of the starch and lessen thickening.
   4. Moisture evaporation may cause thickening and skin formation.
   5. Overcooking and overstirring of tapioca will cause it to become ropy and stringy.

TECHNIQUES APPLICABLE TO QUANTITY COOKERY

C. Prevent Off Flavors
   1. Avoid overproduction with resulting leftovers.
      a. Use standard recipes and yield tables.
      b. Use staggered cookery.
      c. Avoid reheating foods.
      d. Use meat slicers or other labor-saving devices in order to serve promptly.
      e. Avoid long holding of foods.
   2. Use standard recipe for correct proportion of baking powders and baking soda.

PREVENT TEXTURE AND CONSISTENCY CHANGES

A. Starches
   1. Adjust the amount of thickening used in relation to time of holding to prevent undue thickening.
      Examples:
         a. Cream or fruit pie fillings and puddings
         b. Cream soups and sauces
   2. Add egg yolks to flour and sugar mixtures at beginning of cooking period. Use trunnion kettle for cooking.
      Example:
         Cream pie fillings
   3. Add acid to mixtures after cooking and when removed from heat if possible.
      Example:
         Lemon pie
   4. Cover starch mixtures and keep refrigerated.
   5. Avoid overstirring of tapioca and undue evaporation.

B. Gelatin Gels

Gelatin absorbs cold water and swells due to hydration. Upon addition of hot liquid the gelatin dissolves and upon cooling, gelation takes place. The gelation may vary in consistency and stability due to several causes:

1. Amount of gelatin used in relation to holding time.
2. Exposure to air upon holding.
3. Acid concentration if too high affects gelation.
4. The temperature and rate of gelation - gels formed at low temperatures are less stable than those set more slowly - the gelation period should not be forced by putting on ice.
5. Hydrolysis of gelatin by the enzyme in fresh pineapple.

B. Gelatin Gels

1. Use standard amount of gelatin in relation to liquid and to time for holding.
2. Keep gelatin mixtures covered and refrigerated. A damp cloth will prevent evaporation and thickening when necessary to hold.
3. Reduce acid concentration.
   Example:
   Cranberry gelatin
4. Allow time for normal gelation. This time can be cut down and gelation started sooner if only enough liquid is heated to dissolve the gelatin. The addition of the remaining cold liquid will cool the mixture quickly. It should not be necessary to use excess gelatin or to force gelation.
5. Use canned or cooked pineapple when making pineapple salad or dessert.

SCIENTIFIC PRINCIPLES

C. Coagulation

Proteins coagulate when heated. The extent of coagulation depends on:

1. Rate and temperature of coagulation. If proteins are coagulated at too high a temperature or too rapidly, toughening, shrinkage or syneresis takes place.
2. Moisture and long, slow heat will hydrolize the connective tissue without toughening protein.
3. Concentration of protein.
4. Acids and tannins will lower coagulation point and may cause curdling.
5. Salt lowers the coagulation point and affects holding properties.
6. Sugar raises the coagulation point and retards coagulation.
7. Starch is a protective colloid and will prevent overcoagulation of egg.

TECHNIQUES APPLICABLE TO QUANTITY COOKERY

C. Coagulation-Prevent shrinkage and toughening or syneresis.

1. Meats and fish- tender cuts with little connective tissue-use dry heat.
   a. Roast at 300-350° F. to desired degree of doneness. Stagger the roasts for long service periods.
   b. Vary size of roasts for desired doneness as requested by guests. Use meat thermometer to determine degree of doneness.
   c. Broiled meats and fish should be cooked to order.
2. Meats-tough cuts-connective tissue-use moist heat.
   a. Cook at 160-170° F. for a long time.
   b. Stews, pot roasts, swiss steaks should be browned and simmered until tender. Use steamer, stock pots, dutch ovens or ovens.
3. Scrambled Eggs
   a. Dilute the concentration of protein with milk or other liquid.
   b. Cook only to soft curd.
   c. Use a double boiler for large volume. Avoid overstirring.
   d. Cook to order-do not hold on steam table.

4-5. Cream Soups, Creamed or Scalloped Vegetables
   a. Combine cream sauce and vegetable stock just before service. Do not hold on steamtable more than 15 minutes after combining.
   b. Use a binder such as flour or cream sauce to prevent curdling.
   c. Add salt to cream soup just before service.

D. Crystallization

Crystallization is produced when a supersaturated sugar solution is stirred or beaten. As the solution cools, it becomes more highly supersaturated and smaller crystals will be produced upon beating. Finer crystals and a more plastic product may be formed by:

1. Addition of cream of tartar to produce other sugars.
2. Addition of another sugar such as glucose or corn syrup.
3. Preventing evaporation.

6-7. Cream Pie Filling-Puddings

a. Egg yolks mixed with flour and sugar may be added at beginning of cooking period. Cook in double boiler or trunnion.

D. Prevent Crystallization

1. Add extra corn syrup to frostings if they need to be held.
2. Ice only part of cakes if consumption varies. Ice the cakes as needed with fresh icing.
3. Keep frostings covered to prevent crystallization and evaporation.

SCIENTIFIC PRINCIPLES

E. Gluten Formation

Gluten is formed from the proteins in flour when liquid is added and the flour is mixed or kneaded. Gluten formation and length of strands will vary with:

1. Strength of flour-a strong flour will absorb more water and produce more and stronger gluten.
2. The proportion of fat, eggs, sugar and water present.
3. Amount of stirring or mixing. When overmixed there is more of a tendency to form tough, elastic and adhesive gluten strands, especially if mixture is low in fat, sugar or moisture. Gluten particles are sticky and the uneven escape of gas forms tunnels upon baking.
4. Dropping by spoons causes more stretching of strands, causing tunnels.

TECHNIQUES APPLICABLE TO QUANTITY COOKERY

E. To Prevent Gluten Formation

1. Use correct type of flour for batters or doughs to be made.
2. Use a standardized recipe.
3. Avoid overmixing and overbeating by using exact timing. This is especially necessary with use of electric mixers.
   <u>Example</u>:
   Avoid tunnels in muffins
4. Avoid over-handling or dropping by spoonfuls.
   <u>Examples</u>:
   Muffins
   Cakes

F. Foam Formation

1. Egg whites used as leavening depend upon the ability of the protein to surround air bubbles. This is made possible by the coagulation of the egg whites upon beating, giving the foam stability. The foam is unstable at the frothy stage. With continued beating, the foam will peak and there will be less seepage. When beating is continued beyond this stage, the foam will be dry, feather and break. The addition of sugar at the beginning or foamy stage, gives a more stable foam.
2. Foods depending upon the foam for leavening should be cooked at a low temperature and there should be complete heat penetration to prevent syneresis. Baking in a water bath, helps to maintain a low temperature.

F. To Produce Stable Foam

1. Add sugar at the beginning of beating period or when eggs are at foamy stage to avoid overbeating and feathering.

   Examples:
   - Frostings
   - Meringues
2. Stagger the beating of egg whites, the combining with other mixtures and the baking of products when egg whites are used for leavening.

   Examples:
   - Cheese fondue
   - Souffles

SCIENTIFIC PRINCIPLES	TECHNIQUES APPLICABLE TO QUANTITY COOKERY
G. Emulsions Emulsions are formed when small droplets of one liquid are held suspended in another. Most emulsions are not stable unless an emulsifying agent is added. A permanent emulsion is usually formed by using eggs as the emulsifying agent. A more stable emulsion is formed if mixture is well beaten between each addition of oil. A temporary emulsion may be formed by the use of a binder such as paprika or mustard as in French dressing. An emulsion may break if: 1. Insufficient emulsifying agent is used. 2. Oil is added too rapidly. 3. There are too sudden changes in temperature. 4. Evaporation takes place due to improper storage. 5. Added to an acid fruit or moist vegetable mixture.	G. To Form Stable Emulsions 1. Use a standardized recipe and make mayonnaise in quantity. 2. After emulsion is formed, the oil and vinegar may be added in thirds, if well beaten between each addition. 3. Store mayonnaise in covered containers. Keep cool but do not freeze. 4. If emulsion breaks, remake by adding broken emulsion to more egg yolks. 5. Shake temporary emulsions before use.

WILTING AND SHRINKAGE

A. Most foods lose moisture through the permeable walls and will wilt and shrink upon standing.

B. Overcooking causes an undue softening of foods with resulting decrease in volume.

C. The texture of vegetables depend upon sugar content. If too concentrated, the cells lose water and collapse.

D. Overcooking causes sluffing-off of valuable parts.

AVOID WILTING AND SHRINKAGE

A. Use proper buying procedures to prevent long holding.

B. Use proper storage methods.

C. Use careful preparation methods. Avoid overcooking.

Examples:

- Meats will shrink if cooked at high temperatures.
- Overcooked vegetables decrease in volume.
- Whipped eggs lose air.
- Batters lose volume upon standing.

D. Use short holding periods.

1. Use proper equipment for preparation and cooking.
2. Cook at intervals as needed.
3. Serve promptly.

E. Avoid reheating of food by cutting leftovers to a minmum.

Examples:

- Use standard recipes and portions
- Make yield studies
- Make popularity studies

SCIENTIFIC PRINCIPLES	TECHNIQUES APPLICABLE TO QUANTITY COOKERY
TEMPERATURE CHANGES Foods are more acceptable if served at correct temperatures. Hot foods should be served at 130-150° F. and cold foods at 59-60° F.	TO PREVENT TEMPERATURE CHANGES A. Have good floor plans, equipment and distribution and service systems. Example: Tray service in a hospital B. Have cooperation of personnel in serving and distribution of foods. Example: Nursing staff in hospital C. Have well placed facilities for heating and chilling food during service. D. Check temperature losses in large food volumes. Example: Temperature in center of large container of soup E. Have all facilities for service ready when food arrives so that food can be served promptly and at correct temperature.

BACTERIAL CHANGES	TO PREVENT BACTERIAL CHANGES
Bacterial growth may be prevented in raw or cooked foods if:	
A. Pure and uncontaminated foods are purchased.	A. Buy food from safe sources. Examples: Inspected meats Pasteurized milk
B. Foods are not held too long or improperly stored. Some foods are more susceptible to spoilage. Example: The connective tissue around fish incubates bacteria readily causing softening and spoilage.	B. Store food at correct temperatures. Never hold foods at room temperatures even for short periods.
C. Foods are sufficiently and properly cooked. Example: Pork	C. Properly cook all foods.
D. Hot foods are chilled quickly and completely when stored.	D. Cool foods quickly. Store in refrigerator in shallow containers so as to cool to center of mass.
E. Leftovers are kept refrigerated and used promptly.	E. Avoid holding foods over long periods on steamtable and in heated carts. Example: Keep cream pie fillings chilled.
F. Frozen foods are kept frozen and thawed correctly.	F. Keep frozen foods frozen until ready for use. Never thaw and refreeze. Thaw in refrigerator, not at room temperature.

SUGGESTIONS FOR QUANTITY COOKERY TECHNIQUES

This section contains a summary of the previously discussed scientific principles and management techniques applied to the preparation in quantity of some basic foods. If these suggestions are followed, common errors can be prevented or if they do occur, the reasons can be readily determined and future failures avoided.

Suggestions for Quantity Cookery Techniques

SOUPS

<u>Stock Soups</u>

Use shank and bones for soup stock, 2/3 meat, 1/3 bone.
Brown some of meat to get richer flavor and color.
Make soup in a steam-jacketed kettle or stock pot.
Add cold water to meat to extract juices.
Simmer for long time.
Add interesting herbs and seasonings and vegetable waters.
Add raw or cooked vegetables, barley, rice and other foods for added nutrients.
Drain stock. Cool quickly. Keep refrigerated.

<u>Cream Soup</u>

Use white sauce of suitable consistency.
Hold in double boiler or bain marie.
Combine cream sauce and well seasoned vegetable stock as needed.
Combine in relays for long serving periods.
Salt just before serving.
Hold short time on steam table.

FISH AND MEAT

Fish

Keep fish frozen or chilled until ready for use.

Do not thaw at room temperature. Cook in steamer using shallow unperforated pan. If using top of stove, cook gently to avoid agitation. Avoid overcooking. Avoid overhandling. Season with herbs.

Oven fry fish by egging and crumbing and cooking in well greased pans in oven at 400° F.

Stews, Pot Roasts, Swiss Steak

Use moist heat for less tender cuts of meat.

Flour and brown all or part of meat to develop flavor and color.

Use Dutch oven or steam roaster.

Add hot water and simmer for long time.

Do not boil.

Season well and thicken.

Cook vegetables separately and add just before serving.

Hold stews containing vegetables for short time only on steam tables.

Roasts

Use suitable grade and cut.

Roast in thermostatically controlled roasting oven.

Insert a thermometer for internal temperature to indicate degree of doneness.

Roast with fat side up.

Have even circulation of dry heat.

Do not add water or cover.

Roast at 300-350° F. to desired doneness.

Vary size of roasts and stagger the roasting time to give degree of doneness requested by customer.

Roast pork until well done.

Remove from oven 1/2 hour before carving.

Carve carefully and as ordered by customers. If all are to be served at one time, use a meat slicer for efficiency, quality and standard portions.

Weigh standard portions.

Do not carve meat and reheat.

Steaks, Chops

Use dry heat for tender cuts of meat.

Buy fabricated cuts to assure uniform cost and size of serving.

Use electric or charcoal grill or salamander for broiling.

Preheat grill.

Broil at 375-450° F. to desired degree of doneness as requested by customer.

Cook to order - do not hold.

Do not broil pork chops. Brown and braise or egg and crumb and oven broil at 400° F.

MEAT SUBSTITUTES

Eggs

Soft Cooked Eggs
- Use egg cooker or timer.
- Cook eggs to order and to the desired doneness.
- Cook below boiling point.

Hard Cooked Eggs
- Use steamer and perforated pan.
- Cool quickly in running water to prevent discoloration.
- Slice with egg slicer for even slices.

Scrambled Eggs
- Cook to order when possible.
- Cook in double boiler for large groups.
- Undercook rather than overcook.
- Stagger cooking for long service periods.
- Avoid long holding.

Cheese Dishes
- Select well ripened cheese.
- Grate or shred to allow quick melting.
- Cook at 300-350° F. Combine cheese with cooked starch ingredients.
- Stagger the mixing and baking as needed for long service.

Legumes
- Soak overnight.
- Use steamer and unperforated basket - use plenty of water.
- Add soda to cut down cooking time.
- A longer time is needed for softening when acid or molasses is added.
- Bake slowly and only until soft.

Cereals and Starches
- Cook in boiling salted water in unperforated basket or in trunnion kettles in large amount of water.
- Cook quickly until soft but still holds shape.
- Rinse under running water to remove excess starch.
- Avoid long holding after cooking.

Deep Fat Frying

- Use neutral fresh fats with high smoking point for frying - 350-400° F.
- Prepare foods for frying with automatic cutters or slicers to assure even sizes in order to get even doneness and browning.
- Use fryers with thermostatic control and automatic filters and two compartments.
- Keep food for frying at room temperature.
- Avoid overloading baskets.
- Bring fat back to correct temperature before adding more food.
- Fry cooked foods at 375-385° F. to brown and reheat.
- Fry uncooked foods at 350-375° F. to assure cooking before browning.
- Egg and crumb for even brownness and to prevent fat absorption.
- Fry food to order as needed.
- Drain well.
- Keep fryers clean.

VEGETABLE COOKERY

General Vegetable Preparation

Select fresh, good quality vegetables of even size and maturity.
Use wide variety of vegetables.
Store short time and under proper conditions.
Make definite time schedules for preparation.
Use short cuts and machines to reduce preparation time and waste.

General Vegetable Cookery

Use vegetables in natural state or in whole pieces, when possible.
Cover prepared vegetables with damp cloth until ready to cook.
Cook in steamer or trunnion kettles.
Do not cook too much at one time.
Use staggered cookery for long service periods.
Save cooking waters.
Season carefully.
Serve standard portions.

Green Vegetables

Cook in trunnion kettle in salted water.
Cook short time.
Avoid undue agitation in cooking, especially for vegetables with tender tops. Avoid undue handling by tieing in bundles or placing in servings when cooking.
Serve at once or use staggered cookery.
Use shallow pans on steamtable and replenish often.

Cabbage

Select fresh heads of cabbage.
Do not shred and leave exposed to air or water.
Serve in large pieces or wedges when possible.
Cook a short time in steamer in unperforated baskets in salted water, or in trunnion kettles.
Serve at once or use staggered cookery.
Avoid long holding on steam table or in carts.

Onions

Select mild flavored onions.
Cook in steamer in unperforated basket in salted water or in trunnion kettle.
Cook short time.
Use staggered cookery.
Avoid long holding on steamtable.

Frozen Vegetables

Thaw in refrigerator. Do not thaw and refreeze.
Cook frozen vegetables when partially frozen.
Cook shorter time than for fresh vegetables.
Cook as needed for service.
Avoid long holding on steamtable.

Potatoes and Root Vegetables

Use uniform size and shape.
Peel in vegetable peeler when possible.
Avoid overloading peeler.
Run 2-3 minutes only. Avoid overrunning.
Avoid too early preparation and long standing in water.
Avoid unnecessary cutting, peeling and trimming.
Steam in perforated baskets. Cook 15-20 pounds in basket to prevent breakage and to assure heat penetration and even doneness.
Shake basket after removal from steamer to allow the escape of steam and prevent condensation.
Avoid overcooking.

Baked Potatoes

Select mealy potatoes of even size.
Bake at 450° F.
Stagger baking. Split to allow steam to escape.
Serve at once.

Mashed Potatoes

Mash potatoes in mixer using paddle.
Mash while hot - allow steam to escape-add hot milk and butter.
Avoid overmashing.
May use dried milk as a stabilizer.
Stagger the cooking and mashing for long service periods.
Avoid long holding after mashing.

French Fried Potatoes

Use potatoes that have been stored at 60-70° F. for 2-3 weeks to reduce sugar content.
Use French fry cutter.
Soak for a short time in salt water to reduce starch, shorten cooking time and reduce fat absorption.
Dry to prevent decomposition of fat.
Use thermometer or thermostatically controlled electric fryer.
Blanch at 380° F.
Brown just before serving at 400° F. Fry to order.
Do not overload frying baskets.
Drain.
Avoid long holding.

SALADS

Salad Greens

Use fresh, crisp greens of interesting variety.

Trim off outside, bruised leaves of heads of lettuce.

Store heads in refrigerator in polyetheylene bags.

Prepare greens for salads (lettuce cups, hearts or shredded). Handle gently, exert any pressure at root end.

Cover with damp cloth and refrigerate until ready to assemble.

Assemble salads promptly.

Refrigerate until ready for service.

Add appropriate salad dressing just before service.

Fruit and Vegetable Salads

Select fruits and vegetables with contrast of color, shape, texture and flavor.

Design the arrangements.

Prepare all ingredients carefully. Using slicers, shredders and shortcuts to prepare quickly and evenly. Avoid long holding.

Cover ingredients with damp cloth and refrigerate until ready to assemble.

Use assembly line method for combining salads.

Refrigerate until ready to serve.

Potato, Meat, Fish, Egg Salads

Cube all ingredients evenly.

Mix together and marianate for several hours or overnight.

Keep chilled.

Combine with a boiled or combination boiled and mayonnaise dressing to prevent leaking.

Assemble rapidly and keep chilled.

Garnish attractively.

Gelatin Salads

Use correct amount of good quality gelatin for time and water allowed for gelation.

Use less gelatin if to be held overnight. Cover with damp cloth to prevent evaporation.

Dilute high acid concentration.

Shorten congealing time by use of small amount of hot liquid to dissolve gelatin.

Cool with remaining cold liquid.

Allow time for normal gelation.

Do not force by placing on ice.

Add fruits and vegetables or other ingredients after gelatin is partially congealed to prevent layering.

Assemble salads quickly and keep refrigerated.

SALAD DRESSING

French Dressing

- Use correct proportion of oil, vinegar or lemon juice.
- Use interesting herbs and seasonings.
- Use paprika or mustard as stabilizers.
- Mix in electric mixer in quantity and keep on hand.
- Shake before using.
- Add to salads just before serving.

Boiled Dressings

- Use a variety of tested recipes.
- Cook in trunnion kettle until starch is cooked.
- Make in quantity - Cover and refrigerate.
- Add to salads for a binder.
- Use combination boiled and mayonnaise for some salads.

Mayonnaise

- Use ingredients that are at room temperature.
- Make in electric mixer in quantity.
- After emulsion is formed, oil and vinegar can be added 1/3 at a time if beaten well between each addition.
- Keep cool, not chilled.
- Hold in covered containers.
- If emulsion breaks, add broken emulsion to more egg yolks.
- Use as a garnish on salads.
- Combine with boiled dressing for fruit or vegetable salads to prevent leaking.

DESSERTS, CAKES, PIES

Puddings and Cream Pie Fillings

Use standard recipes with correct amount of thickening in relation to time and volume.

Add eggs to starch and sugar mixture-add to hot liquid and cook in trunnion kettle.

Avoid overcooking.

Allow mixture to cool before folding in the whites of eggs.

Add lemon juice after removing mixture from heat for lemon pie.

Refrigerate.

Fruit Pie Fillings

Use correct proportion of ingredients.

Excess sugar will prevent thickening.

Thicken juice in trunnion kettle.

Add fruit.

Place in unbaked shell.

Bake at 450° F.

Pie Crust

Use neutral fat.

Use standard recipe and techniques.

Blend fat and flour in electric mixer, using a pastry blender.

Avoid overmixing and overhandling to prevent development of gluten and loss of air bubbles.

Roll crusts with pie-rolling machine, when possible. Crusts may be rolled ahead and placed in layers and frozen or refrigerated.

Cakes

Use standard recipes and procedures.

Use electric mixer and careful timing. Scrape down bowl. Mix tartrate baking powder, if used, with a little flour and add at end to prevent loss of gas. Use double-acting powder for batters or doughs that need to stand. Keep mixture cool. Weigh amount in pans for baking. Use standard size pans. Cut through batter to even air bubbles. Bake as directed. Place on cake cooler and allow to stand 10 minutes before removal from pans. Use a variety of toppings and frostings. Hold some cakes uniced if consumption varies. Cut in interesting shapes for variety.

Custards

Use standard recipe.

Cook soft custards in double boiler.

Bake custards in water bath to top of custard.

Allow longer baking time if homogenized milk is used.

Use hot milk to cut down baking time.

Bake at 250-300° F.

Meringue

Beat egg whites in electric mixer.

Add sugar at foamy stage or beginning.

Avoid overbeating causing feathering.

Avoid holding after beating.

Place on pie fillings while they are warm, completely covering the filling.

Bake short time at 400° F.

Cool gradually at room temperature.

HOT BREADS

Muffins

Use standard recipes with variations.

Use double acting baking powder in correct proportion.

Mix with electric mixer just beyond the wetting of dry ingredients but not to a smooth mixture.

Pan mixture quickly by using one stroke of a scoop or spoon to fill pans. Do not drop batter into pan.

Use staggered mixing and baking for long service periods.

Bake at 400-425° F.

Serve hot.

Biscuits

Use standard recipes with variations.

Blend fat and flour in electric mixer. Control time of mixing to avoid overmixing.

Roll and cut or bake in sheets and cut after baking.

Refrigerate if dough is to be held before baking. Cover with damp cloth.

Bake at 450° F. Stagger baking as needed for service.

Serve hot.

SUGGESTED REVIEW ON QUALITY

1. Judge finished products by standard rating scales.

2. Analyze any failure in reference to principles involved and suggest corrections of the following:
   a. Curdled cream of asparagus soup
   b. Watery mashed potatoes
   c. Watery scrambled eggs
   d. Curdled scalloped potatoes
   e. Discolored spinach
   f. Leaky salads
   g. Thin lemon pie filling
   h. Cream pies that thin on standing
   i. Coarse grained cakes
   j. Tunnels in muffins
   k. Crystallized frostings
   l. Flat tasting coffee
   m. Broken mayonnaise
   n. Strong cabbage flavor
   o. Layered fruit gelatin

3. Note possible points where special supervision is necessary to prevent failures.

4. Suggest corrections for undesirable results.

5. Explain and apply the principles of meat and vegetable cookery in the making of stew in quantity.

SUGGESTED SHORT STUDIES ON QUALITY

Suggested Short Studies on Color and Appearance Changes

1. Cook a green vegetable, such as spinach, in the ways listed below. Note cooking time, and compare color and quality changes in each case:
   a. In steamer in perforated pan and in water in unperforated pan.
   b. In water on top of stove.
   c. In trunnion kettle.

2. Hold a green vegetable, cooked as indicated, on a steam table for various lengths of time and note color changes. Compare with studies of nutritive and other quality losses.
   a. Cook with water.
   b. Cook covered, without water.
   c. Cook uncovered, without water.

3. Suggest the best method for cooking green vegetables:
   a. To be served all at one time.
   b. To be served over a longer period.

4. Repeat 3, using white and yellow vegetables in various sizes.

5. Cook red cabbage in the following ways and note and compare color changes;
   a. In steam, without water.
   b. In steamer with water.
   c. Cook in acidulated water.
   Hold various products as cooked in (ABC) on steam table and note changes. Suggest recipes to use for red vegetables to prevent discoloration.

BIBLIOGRAPHY

Color and Appearance Change

See Bibliography Nutritive Losses, Page 90
See Bibliography Quality in Quantity Food - General, Page 92

Noble, Isabel and Gordon, Jane. Ascorbic Acid and Color Retention in Green Beans Cooked by Different Methods. Journal of the American Dietetic Association. Vol. 32, pp. 119, Feb. 1956.

Longree, Karla. Discoloration of Machine Peeled Potatoes. Journal of the American Dietetic Association. Vol. 32, pp. 639, July 1956.

Suggested Studies on Flavor

1. Note flavor changes in coffee:
   a. Made from different grinds.
   b. Made by different methods.
   c. Made in different quantities in the urns.
   d. Held for various lengths of time.

2. Suggest best procedures to follow for tearoom, cafeteria, or dormitory service on basis of results secured in (1).

3. Squeeze oranges or grapefruit and allow juice to stand in refrigerator, covered and uncovered for short periods and overnight. Note flavor changes. What procedures would you suggest?

4. Check flavor losses after:
   a. Overcooking celery.
   b. Cooking carrots in large quantity of water.
   c. Cooking carrots in large quantity of water to which sugar has been added.

5. Note flavor changes in strong flavored vegetables.
   a. Cook turnips or strong onions in steamer with water and without water for various lengths of time. Compare flavor. Suggest best method and time for cooking.
   b. Repeat above experiment, using white and yellow onions. Compare and suggest proper procedures.
   c. Hold on the steam table a strong juice vegetable that has been properly cooked for varying periods. Note any flavor change.

6. Cook bacon on rack in oven and in skillet on top of stove. Compare flavor and time.

7. Suggest flavor studies in other foods.

BIBLIOGRAPHY

Flavor Loss and Change

Simpson, Jean and Evelyn Halliday. The Behavior of Sulphur Compounds in Vegetables on Cooking. Journal of Home Economics, Vol. 20, pp. 121. February, 1928.

Porter, Thelma, et al. Changes in Fats During Frying. Industrial Engineering Chemistry, Vol. 22, pp. 811. 1932.

Vaile, Gladys E. and Luella O'Neill. Certain Factors Which Affect the Palatability and Cost of Roast Beef Served in Institutions. Journal of the American Dietetic Association, Vol. 13, pp. 34-39. May, 1937.

Watts, Betty M. Flavor in Foods. Journal of Home Economics, Vol. 31, pp. 673-679. December, 1939.

Isker, Rohland A. Notes on the Use and Effects of Monosodium Glutamate. Journal of the American Dietetic Association, Vol. 25, pp. 760-763. September, 1949.

Suggested Studies on Consistency Changes

1. Make a chocolate pie. Cut it and check consistency.
   1 hour after making
   4 hours after making
   After it stands overnight

2. Make gelatin according to a standard recipe. Check at various periods and note changes.

3. Make a cream sauce, add salt, and hold all morning in a double boiler. Note any coagulation or curdling.

4. Make a cream of tomato soup and let stand on steam table during entire serving period. Note changes.

5. Add cream sauce to aspargus and hold. Note curdling. Repeat, using celery. Explain any changes.

6. Make scrambled eggs in double boiler and in skillet. Hold each and note changes at various periods. Note relative time and ease of each method.

7. Make various types of icings and note the crystallization at different periods.

8. Make a study of beef stew by checking the standard product with a sample that has been held on steam table.

BIBLIOGRAPHY

Consistency and Texture Changes

Lowe, Belle. Experimental Cookery. New York: John Wiley and Sons.

Nason, Edith. Introduction to Experimental Cookery. New York: McGraw-Hill Book Company, Inc.

Sweetman, Marion D. Food Preparation. New York: John Wiley and Sons.

Meuser, Mary. Factors Determining the Quality of White Sauce in Large Quantity Cookery. Journal of Home Economics, Vol. 14, pp. 575. November, 1922.

Billings, Mary N., Alice M. Briant, Karla Longree, and Katharine W. Harris. Cream Pie Fillings Prepared in Multiples of an Eight-Pie Batch. Journal of the American Dietetic Association, Vol. 28, pp. 228-230. March, 1952.

Rose, Thelma, Martha Dresslar and Kathleen A. Johnston. The Effect of the Method of Fat and Water Incorporation on the Average Shortness and the Uniformity of Tenderness of Pastry. Journal of Home Economics, Vol. 44, pp. 707. November, 1952.

Nielsen, Hester J., Jean D. Hewitt and Natalie K. Fitch. Factors Influencing Consistency of a Lemon-Pie Filling. Journal of Home Economics, Vol. 44, pp. 782. December, 1952.

Longree, Karla. Muffins Prepared from Soft Wheat Flour. Journal of the American Dietetic Association, Vol. 29, pp. 765-769. August, 1953.

Longree, Karla. Viscosity of White Sauces Prepared in Quantity. Journal of the American Dietetic Association, Vol. 29, pp. 997-1003. October, 1953.

Suggested Short Studies on Wilting and Shrinkage

1. Check the weights of meat loaf before and after baking at high and low temperatures.

2. Check the shrinkage of several brands of sausage.

3. Check loss in weight of servings of meat after holding.

4. Check shrinkage from hamburger as purchased and from meat ground from specified ingredients.

5. Make up a tossed or vegetable salad and add dressing to it at different periods. Note volume and relative number of servings.

6. Check volume of spinach or other green vegetables after holding for long periods on steam table.

BIBLIOGRAPHY

Wilting and Shrinkage

Shircliffe, Arnold. Quantity Cookery. Journal of the American Dietetic Association, Vol. 7, pp. 272-276. December, 1931.

Alexander, Lucy and O. G. Hankins. Yield and Quality of Cooked Edible Portion of Smoked Hams. Journal of the American Dietetic Association, Vol. 28, pp. 636-639. July, 1952.

Armour and Company. "Meat for Quantity Cookery". Chicago.

National Livestock and Meat Board. "Meat and Meat Cookery". 1942.

Lancaster, Mable and Marion Sweetman. The Relation of Maturity, Size, Period of Storage and Variety to the Speed and Cooking Evenness of Cooking potatoes. Journal of Home Economics, Vol. 24, pp. 262-268. March, 1932.

Pfund, Marion. Some Objective Tests on Potatoes. Journal of Home Economics, Vol. 30, pp. 554. October, 1938.

Wood, Marion. Potatoes in Institution Food Service. Cooking Qualities, Waste in preparation, Buyers Preferences and Practices. Cornell University Agricultural Experimental Station Bulletin 798. March, 1943.

Kirkpatrick, Mary, Beatrice M. Mountjoy and Linda Albright. Influence of Variety on Yield of Potatoes Prepared for Cooking. Journal of the American Dietetic Association, Vol. 28, pp. 231. March, 1952.

Suggested Short Studies on Temperature Changes

1. Make a study of the internal temperature of canned goods or soup when it leaves the kitchen and at different intervals during the service period. Check with standards.

2. Taste foods at different temperatures, and note the relation between flavor and temperature.

3. Make a list of foods that can be served in institutions without much loss of temperature.

BIBLIOGRAPHY

Temperature Changes

Denton, Minna. Internal Temperatures of Foods During Cooking. Journal of Home Economics. Vol. 14, pp. 579. November 1922.

Wertman, Zoe Dorthy. Analysis of Actual Food Temperatures. Master's Thesis. University of Chicago.

Carden, Grace and Eleanor Mussey. A Study of the Temperature at Which Foods May be Served to Hospital Patients When Insulated Food Conveyors are Used. Journal of the American Dietetic Association. Vol.7, pp. 27. June 1931.

Suggested Short Studies on Bacterial Growth

From your readings:
1. List foods most subject to bacterial growth.
2. Indicate the care that should be given to each.

BIBLIOGRAPHY

Bacteriological Changes

Harding, T. Swann. Poisons in Food, Fantasy or Fact. Journal of the American Dietetic Association, Vol. 14, pp. 436. June-July, 1938.

Husseman, Dorothy L. and Fred W. Tanner. New Aspects of the Food Poisoning Problem. Journal of the American Dietetic Association, Vol. 23, pp. 16-21. January, 1947.

Rice, Thurman. Epidemiology of the Dining Table. Journal of the American Dietetic Association, Vol. 23, pp. 22-24. January, 1947.

Black, Lois and Martha Lewis. Effect on Bacterial Growth of Various Methods of Cooling Cooked Foods. Journal of the American Dietetic Association, Vol. 24, pp. 399. May, 1948.

Husseman, Dorothy L. Effect of Cooking on the Bacteriologic Flora of Selected Frozen Precooked Foods. Journal of the American Dietetic Association, Vol. 27, pp. 855. October, 1951.

Ice, Rachel, Karla Longree, Faith Fenton and Katharine Harris. Effect of Holding on Bacterial Count and Palatability of Meat Loaves. Journal of the American Dietetic Association, Vol. 28, pp. 325. April, 1952.

Lewis, Martha, Harry Weiser and A. R. Winter. Bacterial Growth in Chicken Salad. Journal of the American Dietetic Association, Vol. 29, pp. 1094-1099. November, 1953.

Longree, Karla, and White, James C. Cooking Rates and Bacterial Growth in Food Prepared and Stored in Quantity. Journal of the American Dietetic Association. Vol. 31, pp. 124. February, 1955.

Brown, Esther. Handling Pork to Prevent Trichinosis. Journal of the American Dietetic Association. Vol. 32, pp. 802. September, 1956.

Wiedeman, Kathleen et al. Effect of Delayed Cooking on Bacteria in Meat Loaf. Journal of the American Dietetic Association. Vol. 32, pp. 935. October, 1956.

Wiedeman, Kathleen et al. Effect of Holding Time on Bacteria. Journal of the American Dietetic Association. Vol. 33, pp. 37. January, 1957.

Suggestions for Long Problems on Quality in Quantity Food

1. From your studies and reading, make a chart indicating time, method, temperature and serving procedures for quantity cookery that will best preserve nutritive value and other qualitative values in all common vegetables.

   Indicate whether these procedures will vary for food service in the following institutions and how:
   (a) Hospitals (b) Cafeterias (c) Dormitories (d) Tearooms

2. Suggest a study that could be made in any unit to determine timing and amount of any food needing "staggered cookery" during a service period.

3. Make a study of various techniques in the cooking and serving of food in your food service unit or in others visited. Refer to the literature, and indicate possible nutritive losses.

4. Make a study of the possible uses of potatoes cooked with the skins on. Make a comparative study of the nutritive value of potatoes baked at a low and a high temperature.

5. Follow one vegetable through various processes, and check with literature for possible nutritive losses.

6. Make a series of studies, indicating the possible uses and limitations of the pressure steamer and the steam-jacketed kettle in quantity cookery. Give complete instructions regarding techniques to be followed.

7. (a) Make a chart showing the proportions of thickening agents (flour, cornstarch) to use for different holding periods.
   (b) Carry out a similar study for gelatin mixtures.

8. Outline a study that could be made in an institution to check possible temperature losses due to service and food distribution methods.

9. Make a careful study of the reworking of a leftover food--considering the factors of original cost, shrinkage, added ingredients, time and selling price.

10. Show in what ways the techniques as applied to quantity cookery are consistent with the previous discussion or scientific principles.

11. Review literature on nutritive losses in quantity cookery on certain foods.

BIBLIOGRAPHY ON NUTRITIVE LOSSES

Fenton, Faith, Vitamin C as a Criterion of Quality and Nutritive Value in Vegetables. Journal of the American Dietetic Association, Vol. 10, pp. 524-535. June-July, 1940.

Fitch, Natalie K. That Elusive Nutritive Value. Journal of the American Dietetic Association, Vol. 18, pp. 310-312. May, 1942.

Vaile, Gladys. The Effect of Processing Upon the Nutritive Value of Food. Journal of the American Dietetic Association, Vol. 18, pp. 569-574. September, 1942.

Porter, Mame Tanner. Policies, Procedures and Standards of Public Institutions. Journal of the American Dietetic Association, Vol. 18, pp. 825-830. December, 1942.

Nagel, Albert and Robert Harris. Effect of Restaurant Cookery and Service on Vitamin Content of Foods. Journal of the American Dietetic Association, Vol. 19, pp. 23-35. January, 1943.

Daum, Kate, Mary Aimone and Stella Hollister. Ascorbic Acid in Institutional Food. Journal of the American Dietetic Association, Vol. 19, pp. 693. October, 1943.

Kahn, Ruth and Evelyn Halliday. Ascorbic Acid Content of White Potatoes as Affected by Cooking and Standing on the Steam Table. Journal of the American Dietetic Association, Vol. 20, pp. 220-221. April, 1944.

Scoular, Florence and Helen Willard. Effect of Refrigeration on Ascorbic Acid Content of Canned Fruit Juices After Opening. Journal of the American Dietetic Association, Vol. 20, pp. 223. April, 1944.

Brown, Josephine, et al. Ascorbic Acid, Thiamin and Riboflavin in Quick Frozen Broccoli in Institution Food Service. Journal of the American Dietetic Association, Vol 20, pp. 369. June, 1944.

Hinman, Winifred, et al. The Nutritive Value of Canned Foods; VI. Effect of Large-Scale Preparation for Serving on Ascorbic Acid, Thiamin and Riboflavin Content of Commercially Canned Vegetables. Journal of the American Dietetic Association, Vol. 20, pp. 752. December, 1944.

Cutlar, Kathleen, et al. Ascorbic Acid, Thiamin and Riboflavin Retention in Fresh Spinach In Institution Food Service. Journal of the American Dietetic Association, Vol. 20, pp. 757. December, 1944.

Kramer, Martha. Ascorbic Acid Content of Food Served to Army Students. Journal of the American Dietetic Association, Vol. 21, pp. 348. June, 1945.

Schauss, Virginia. Ascorbic Acid Content of Fruits and Vegetables Used in an Institution. Journal of the American Dietetic Association, Vol. 21, pp. 364. June, 1945.

Fenton, F. Retention of Vitamin Values in Large Scale Food Service. Institute of Food Technologists: Proceedings 1945. Champaign, Illinois: The Garrard Press.

Wood, Marion, et al. The Effect of Large-Scale Preparation on Vitamin Retention in Cabbage. Journal of the American Dietetic Association, Vol. 22, pp. 677-682. August, 1946.

Kelley, Louise, et al. Palatability and Ascorbic Acid Retention of Rutabaga, Peas and Cabbage After Holding on Steam Table. Journal of the American Dietetic Association, Vol. 23, pp. 120. February, 1947.

Brinkman, E.V.S., et al. Effect of Various Cooking Methods Upon Subjective Qualities and Nutritive Values of Vegetables. Food Research. Vol. 7, pp. 300. October, 1942.

Watt, Bernice and Margaret Attaya. Vitamin Retention in Quantity Cookery of Vegetables. Journal of Home Economics, Vol. 37, pp. 340. June, 1945.

Wilcox, Ethelyn and Alice Neilson. Effect of Quantity Preparation on the Ascorbic Acid Content of Cabbage Salad. Journal of the American Dietetic Association, Vol. 23, pp. 223. March, 1947.

Fincke, Margaret, et al. Ascorbic Acid Content of Foods as Served. Journal of the American Dietetic Association, Vol. 24, pp. 957. November, 1948.

Causey, Kathryn and Faith Fenton. Effect of Reheating on Palatability, Nutritive Value, and Bacterial Count of Frozen Cooked Foods. I. Vegetables. Journal of the American Dietetic Association, Vol. 27, pp. 491. June, 1951. II. Meat Dishes. Journal of the American Dietetic Association, Vol. 27, pp. 491. June, 1951.

Vinacke, Winifred R. The Effect of Storage, Washing and Cooking on Thiamine Content of Rice. Journal of the American Dietetic Association, Vol. 43, pp. 641. October, 1951.

Westerman, Beulah D. Influence of Storage Time and Temperature on the Vitamins in Pork Roasts. Journal of the American Dietetic Association, Vol. 28, pp. 331. April, 1952.

Charles, Virginia and Frances O. Van Duyne. Comparison of Fresh Frozen Concentrated, Canned Concentrated and Canned Orange Juices. Journal of the American Dietetic Association, Vol. 28, pp. 534. June, 1952.

Walker, Georgianna R. and Polgieter, Martha, Effect of Salt on Ascorbic Acid in Cabbage During Cooking. Journal of the American Dietetic Association. Vol. 32, pp. 821, Sept. 1956

BIBLIOGRAPHY ON QUALITY IN QUANTITY FOOD

General

Fowler and West. Food for Fifty. New York: John Wiley and Sons.

Halliday and Noble. Hows and Whys of Cooking. Chicago: The University of Chicago Press.

Lowe, Belle. Experimental Cookery. Third Edition. New York: John Wiley and Sons.

Miller and Barnhart. Essentials of Food Preparation. Dubuque, Iowa: William C. Brown Company.

Nason. Introduction to Experimental Cookery. New York: McGraw-Hill Book Company.

Sweetman, Marion, and Ingeborg MacKellar. Food Selection and Preparation. Fourth Edition. New York: John Wiley and Sons.

West and Wood. Food Service in Institutions. Second Edition. New York: John Wiley and Sons.

American Home Economics Association. Handbook of Food Preparation. 1954.

Articles

Shircliffe, Arnold. Quantity Cookery. Journal of the American Dietetic Association, Vol. 7, pp. 272-276. December, 1931.

Halliday, Evelyn, and Isabel Noble. Recent Developments in the Science of Cooking. Journal of the American Dietetic Association, Vol. 8, pp. 1-24, May, 1932.

Casteen, Marie L. Quality in Quantity Cookery. Journal of the American Dietetic Association, Vol. 15, pp. 154-163. March, 1939.

Smith, Grace E. Important Factors in Successful Food Service. Journal of the American Dietetic Association, Vol. 15, pp. 557-561, June-July, 1941.

Porter, Mame Tanner. Policies, Procedures, and Standards of Public Institutions. Journal of the American Dietetic Association, Vol. 18, pp. 825-830, December, 1942.

Wickliffe, Capt. Nell. Quality Food Preparation and Service in a Large Army Hospital. Journal of the American Dietetic Association, Vol. 21, pp. 368-377, June, 1945.

Terrell, Margaret. Quality Food Production in College Residence Halls. Journal of the American Dietetic Association, Vol. 21, pp. 446-450, July-August, 1945.

Lewis, Martha. Food Production in General Hospitals. Journal of the American Dietetic Association, Vol. 21, pp. 450-452, July-August, 1945.

Morrissey, Veronica. Quality Food Production in A Commercial Tearoom. Journal of the American Dietetic Association, Vol. 21, pp. 452-454, July-August, 1945.

Simpson, Jean. Frozen Foods for Institution Use. Journal of the American Dietetic Association, Vol. 22, pp. 661-664, August, 1946.

Hart, Constance. Trends in Food Standards. Journal of the American Dietetic Association, Vol. 22, pp. 896-902, October, 1946.

Mitchell, Margaret. Production Management in Today's Kitchen. Journal of the American Dietetic Association, Vol. 23, pp. 25-30, January, 1947.

Jeffs, Kathleen. A Matter of Good Taste. Journal of the American Dietetic Association, Vol. 23, pp. 777-779, September, 1947.

Fields, John A. Development of High Quality Foods. Journal of the American Dietetic Association, Vol. 25. May, 1949.

Aldrich, Pearl Jackson. Quality Food Means More than Recipes. Journal of the American Dietetic Association, Vol. 29, pp. 1089-1093. November, 1953.

Mitchell, Margaret L., Management and Organization in Quality Food Production. Journal of the American Dietitic Association. Vol. 31, pp. 680, July 1955.

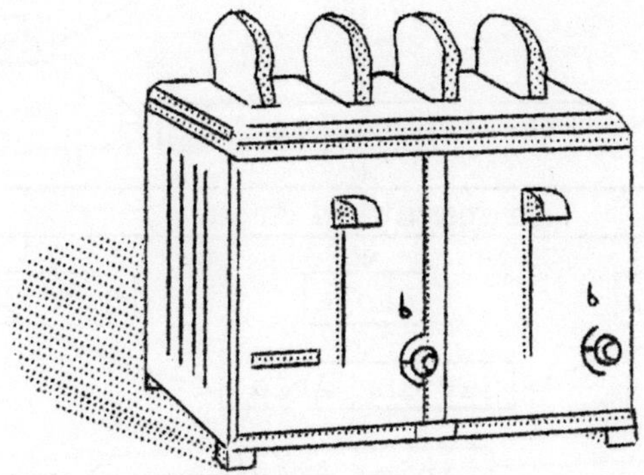

Chapter IV

MODERN AND MECHANIZED FOOD UNITS

Modern and mechanized food units imply good floor planning and the wise selection, use and care of equipment and machines. To produce food in quantity efficiently, the floor plan must be well arranged for preparation and service. The equipment must not be outmoded, inadequate, in poor working condition or inconveniently located. Architects, engineers, dietitians and food managers should all work together to plan, provide and maintain efficient work units.

Floor Plans

The following points should be emphasized in planning a food service unit.

1. Proper orientation in the building
   Is it convenient for guests, receiving of supplies and entrance of workers?
2. Forward flow of all food from receiving, storage, preparation, serving, dining
3. Proper sequence of operations with no retracing of steps
4. No crossing of lines
5. Sufficient space and equipment to accomplish best the work to be done
6. Well planned service areas and a direct and efficient food distribution system to prevent undue holding of food after preparation

A TYPICAL FLOW CHART

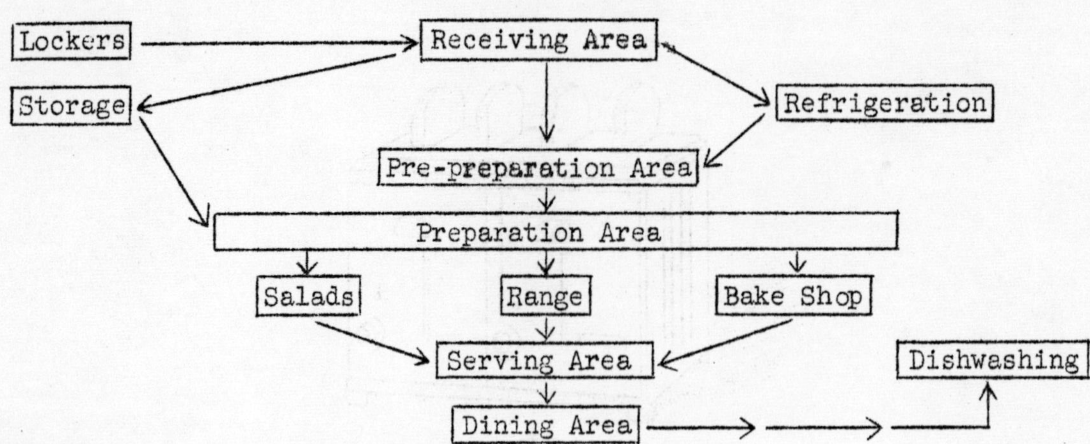

Suggested Problem

Examine your food unit to see if you could rearrange or remodel for more efficiency.

MECHANIZED EQUIPMENT

Modern and suitable equipment in good working condition is essential for control in management. The elimination of some of the human element leads to greater efficiency and to more standardization of output and quality. This need in no way detract from the attractiveness of the product. By eliminating many inefficiencies and "margins of error" more time can be devoted to achieving high food quality and finesse in garnish and service.

The effectiveness of any machine will depend on its wise selection, use, care and upkeep. The need for the machine must be established and knowledge of its performance should be acquired before selection is made.

In this manual it will be possible to give only a few suggestions on the selection, use and care of equipment. References on these topics will be found at the end of the chapter.

Selection of Equipment

1. Establish need.
   Will it be used at least an hour a day?
2. Select a suitable size and model.
   What electric current or steam pressure does it need and is this available?
   Is space needed for machine available?
   Is the size of machine suitable for work to be done?
   Usually an inferior product is produced in an oversize machine. It is also needless expenditure to buy too large a machine.

Example:
Five gallons of coffee made in a ten gallon urn will be inferior.

3. Check durability.
Will it hold up?
Can it be easily repaired?
Can parts be replaced?
Is it easy and safe to operate?
Is it easily cleaned?
Does it meet the needs?
Are results satisfactory?

Advantages of Machines in Quantity Food Production

1. Standardization of product as to form, size and quantity. Uneven portions result in guest dissatisfaction, loss of money and unattractive products. Any machine or piece of equipment that eliminates this variation will be an asset.

Examples:
Slicing machine for bread and meat
French fry cutters
Butter cutters
Shredders
Pie-rolling machine
Standard serving spoons

2. Standardization of product as to quality.
In most organizations there is considerable shifting of personnel. The use of machines, both large and small, will reduce or eliminate the variable in quality during the learning period of a new worker and will make last minute or "staggered cookery" possible.

Examples:
Automatic toasters, egg cookers
Thermometers
Thermostatically controlled ovens, dishwashers

3. Simplification of work
Any piece of equipment which will increase the output during any given period and which will, at the same time, decrease fatigue, is an aid to work simplification. This equipment decreases the number of operations, the kind of operations, or the energy consumed in performing any given task. The real test is the number of clock hours saved. Often a machine can do in one hour what it would take five hours to do by hand. The use of machines often reduces the number of pans in use and also conserves space. In calculating the time, the cleaning up of the machine should be included.

Examples:
Mixing machines
Apple peelers
Dishwashers
Steamers
Slicing machines

4. Increase in volume

   Most power driven machines will increase the volume and will decrease the waste, resulting in greater yields and increased profits.

   Examples:
   Mixing machines increase volume of mashed potatoes, eggs.
   Potato parer reduces the waste if not overloaded or overrun.

5. Improvement in quality

   By proper use of machines and large equipment, the quality of the product far exceeds that of the products made by hand.

   Examples:
   Potatoes are fluffier and smoother than when mashed by hand.
   Cake has improved grain.
   Coffee made in urn retains flavor.
   Dishes washed by machine are better sterilized.

6. Conservation of nutritive value

   Many machines, when properly used, are effective in conserving nutritive value. The minerals and vitamins are retained since there is less shrinkage and the handling and holding time is shortened.

   Examples:
   Potato peeler
   Steam as fuel
   Slicing and shredding machines

7. Improvement in cost control

   By standardizing size, yield, methods, and quality, there is more opportunity to control the cost of raw materials, labor and yield. By careful checks it is possible to determine the number of orders to be obtained from a given quantity, and the output per hour for any given worker. In this way, the exact cost can be anticipated with little variation from day to day.

   Examples:
   Checking machines
   Tabulators
   Dispensing machines

8. Betterment of working conditions

   A well-equipped mechanized factory attracts and holds good workers. Food service units, if they are to compete on the labor market must improve their working conditions. It is good psychology as well as good economics to give a worker the right tools with which to work. Not only does he become more efficient but often a more intelligent class of worker is attracted and labor turnover is lessened.

SUGGESTIONS FOR USE AND CARE OF EQUIPMENT

Most firms issue instructions for the use and care of the machine when purchased. These directions should be posted near the machine and the worker should be trained to follow them. Special instructions on accident prevention should be given.

All recipes should include full directions as to time, volume, speed, temperature, and any other specific information for the correct functioning of the machine. See bibliography on recipes.

All workers should be given specific instructions on the use and care of all equipment used. The "job breakdown" form for instruction is considered the best. It is wise in teaching a student or worker, to use written instructions, demonstrations, movies and other visual aids, followed by sufficient practice and supervision. See bibliography on equipment at the end of chapter.

The machinery may be suitable and well selected but if not properly operated and cared for both the nutritive value and quality of the product may be affected.

A discussion of some of the precautions necessary in the use of specific equipment follows:

FOOD MIXERS

Review general directions for use and care of equipment.

To produce superior quality products when mixing, beating, or whipping by machine use:

1. Proper size bowl and attachments to prevent overmixing. An adapter may be used if volume varies.

   Example:
   Forty or sixty quart mixer is not suitable for twenty quarts of mixture.

2. Proper type and size of attachment

3. Directions for timing to avoid overmixing

4. Directions as to order or method of combining ingredients

   Example:
   Tartrate baking powder is usually added last.

Suggested Studies on Mixer

1. Make a study of yield of egg whites beaten by hand or machine. Extend this study to other foods. Use a bar graph chart to show percent of increase in volume.

2. Make the adjustments that would be necessary in changing from hand method to machine method.

3. Run an experiment using different types of baking powders when using a machine.

4. Suggest other studies.

VEGETABLE PEELERS

Review general directions for use of vegetable peeler.

Peeling vegetables by machine is more pleasant for workers. To save time, reduce waste and preserve nutritive value, take the following precautions:

1. Use a machine that is not too large for volume of vegetables to be peeled.

   Example:
   A fifteen pound machine filled to capacity will result in less loss and there will be less danger of overrunning than fifteen pounds of potatoes run in a large machine.

2. Run vegetables only until skins have been removed. Avoid overrunning with the resultant loss of vegetables and nutritive value.

3. Select vegetables of even size and shape.

4. Keep machine clean.

Suggested Studies on Vegetable Peeler

1. Make a time, waste and cost study on potatoes peeled by hand and those peeled by machine.

2. Test out efficiency and relative waste in using potatoes of uniform size versus uneven shapes and sizes.

3. Use the potato peeler for different types of root vegetables.

4. Make a time study of the efficiency of various volumes in machine at one time.

5. Make a study of time it takes to clean the potato peeler.

6. Suggest other studies.

COFFEE URN

Review directions for use of urn.

To assure the best quality of coffee with the minimum loss of flavor, the following precautions should be followed:

1. Use an urn that is of suitable size for amount of coffee to be made to avoid loss of flavor.

2. Keep coffee urn and bags absolutely clean.

3. Select a well blended urn grind coffee. The proportion of coffee to water varies with the strength, blend, and roast of the coffee used. For average strength, use one pound to two and a half gallons of water.

4. Use fresh boiling water when making coffee and be sure that the hot water in the jacket is at the same level as the coffee in the urn. Never allow the coffee to boil after making. All modern urns are thermostatically controlled to prevent this.

5. Coffee should never stand more than thirty minutes after making. If serving over a long period, twin urns should be used and the coffee remade at well timed intervals.

Suggested Studies on Use of Coffee Urn

1. Make a study of the optimum time for holding coffee after making. Test at different holding periods.

2. Use different grades and grinds in making coffee, noting relative yield and quality.

3. Make different volumes in urn and note quality at different holding periods.

4. Suggest other studies.

USE OF STEAM FOR QUANTITY COOKERY

Steam when used as fuel is clean, inexpensive and a time saver. Steam condenses rapidly when it reaches the cold raw food, thus releasing the full capacity of heat. Condensation decreases as the food becomes warmer and near the temperature of steam. The cooking starts at once. For steam cooking it is necessary to have steam under pressure (3-10 lbs. per sq. inch). The temperature ranges from 185° to 230° C.. Steam and steam equipment is suitable for most quantity cookery when used correctly and carefully controlled. The effect of steam on the preservation of nutrients and its effect on color, flavor and texture have been discussed in chapter three. In all cases it has been found that when the proper methods and timing have been used that steam is a decided aid.

1. Compartment Steamers

Review general directions for use and care of steamers.

Most steamers are equipped with shallow, deep, perforated and unperforated baskets. Knowing when to use each of these will materially affect the quality and nutritive value of food being cooked. Suggestions for their use follows:

a. Foods needing long slow cooking such as tongue, fowl, or ham, cook in water in an unperforated basket.
b. Root vegetables needing quick heat penetration, cook in perforated baskets. Avoid breakage and loss by not filling basket too full. A ten pound maximum is amount recommended for each basket.
c. Green vegetables cook in a shallow basket and usually in small amount of water for a very short time. The trunnion kettle is generally considered preferable to the compartment steamer for green vegetables.
d. Strong juice vegetables cook in a shallow unperforated pan in water. Avoid overcooking.
e. Flour mixtures cook under lower steam pressure at start and avoid having the mixture too moist.
f. Legumes, dried fruits and cereals, cook in water in unperforated basket. Water evaporation will need to be watched.

2. Trunnion and Steam Jacketed Kettles

Cooking is done by live steam and in an open kettle, thus the heat penetration is quick and complete. The water for cooking comes quickly to the boil, both before and after adding material to be cooked. The use of these kettles is especially good for "staggered cooking" of vegetables. Even though water is used for cooking, there is little destruction of nutritive value because the cooking time is so short. Steam kettles are also very good for cooking pie fillings, flour mixtures, fowl, ham, soup stock and other foods needing long cooking, if the following precautions are taken.

a. Avoid too much steam pressure causing agitation.
b. Avoid overcooking flour or cornstarch mixtures, since evaporation is fast.
c. Avoid overcooking around the edges.

3. Steam Tables and Heated Carts

Steam tables or carts can be used for holding food for short periods of time. They should never be used for cooking food. Foods should be put in shallow containers and these should be replenished every fifteen minutes.

Tables heated by electricity and thermostatically controlled are more efficient than the steam table.

Electrically heated carts are excellent for transportation of food, but long holding periods should be avoided. See references on quality food.

Suggested Studies on Use of Steam for Quantity Cooking

1. Define the principles of steam cooking.

2. Test the use of steam for various foods and check relative merits as to color, flavor, texture, shrinkage and time.

3. Make a time chart for use of steamer for various foods.

4. Make a chart for methods of using steam for cooking various foods.

5. Check relative merits of cooking various foods:
   a. In steamer in water.
   b. Without water.
   c. In perforated or unperforated basket.
   d. As to time and relative merits of shallow and deep baskets.
   e. Compare the flavor of cabbage or onions cooked in water and without water.
   f. Cook for varying lengths of time and chart results.
   g. Compare steam cooking of equal amount of potatoes as to time and results with top of stove cooking.
   h. Make comparative studies as to time and quality of food cooked in a steamer, on top of stove, and in the trunnion kettle.
   i. Attempt to cook a sugar solution for frosting in a trunnion kettle. Explain results.
   j. What is the main problem in cooking a cornstarch or egg mixture in a trunnion kettle?

6. Hold food on steam table and check quality at intervals: thirty minutes; one hour; two hours.

7. Check temperature of food when it comes to service table and at various intervals.

8. Check time as food leaves main kitchen and when it arrives at patient's room or in a private dining room or banquet hall. Chart quality and temperature losses.

Short Problems on Machines and Equipment

1. Chart the relative advantages of the use of each piece of equipment or machinery used in quantity cookery. Give data from studies on time, shrinkage, waste, standardization, quality and cost.

2. Study the possible abuses in the use of the equipment and machinery used in quantity cookery that will affect the quality of the food produced.

3. Study the accident control factor on each piece of equipment.

4. List small pieces of equipment you have used:
   a. Which have improved quality? How?
   b. Which have aided standardization? How?
   c. Which have simplified work? How?

5. Outline daily and periodic care for the maintenance of various types of equipment.

6. Suggest other problems.

Suggestions for Term Papers on Machines and Equipment

1. Compare the time, waste, cost, and quality of food prepared by hand or by power-driven machinery.
   Example: Potato peeling

2. Analyze cost of a food or recipe in light of labor costs due to poor techniques, instruction, equipment, or training. Restudy when above has been corrected.

3. Select a process that is being poorly done. Work out a new method. Retrain workers to use new method.

4. Study the use of machinery and large equipment and the efficiency of their use in typical sororities or fraternities or other small units.

5. Work out a complete instruction chart for cooking all types of vegetables in quantity.

6. Work out a complete instruction chart for the method and equipment to use in cooking other foods by use of steam.

7. Outline and carry out a training period for a worker who has not used a machine and is not interested in doing it.

8. Analyze what any given machine can do and run experiments to see that they fulfull their performance expectancy.

9. Suggest other topics.

BIBLIOGRAPHY ON EQUIPMENT

American Dietetic Association. Care of Food Service Equipment. Minneapolis: Burgess Publishing Company.

Clawson, Augusta. Equipment Maintenance Manual. New York: Ahrens Publishing Company.

West, Bessie and LeVelle Wood. Food Service in Institutions. New York: John Wiley and Sons.

Fowler, Sina and Bessie Brooks West. Food for Fifty. New York: John Wiley and Sons.

Getting the Most from Steam Cooking. Cleveland Range Company. Cleveland, Ohio.

Cooking the Modern Way with Steam Jacketed Kettles. Groen Manufacturing Company. Chicago, Illinois.

Whiteman, Elizabeth Fuller and Florance B. King. A Study of the Waste in Preparation and in Cooking of Fresh Vegetables and the Fuel Consumed. Journal of the American Dietetic Association, Vol. 14, pp. 615-622, October, 1938.

Handy, Etta H. Modern Equipment for Food Service. Journal of the American Dietetic Association, Vol. 17, pp. 551-556, June-July, 1941.

Francis, Kent. Relation of Work Habits to Receipts. American Restaurant Association, April, 1943.

Simpson, Jean I. Frozen Foods for Institutional use. Journal of the American Dietetic Association, Vol. 22, pp. 661-664, August, 1946.

Bollman, Marion; Sadie Brenner, Lois Gordon and Mary Eck Lambert. Application of Electronic Cooking to Large Scale Feeding. Journal of the American Dietetic Association, Vol. 24, pp. 1041, December, 1948.

Thomas, Miriam Higgins; Sadie Brenner, Adaline Eaton, and Virginia Craig. Effect of Electronic Cooking on Nutritive Value of Foods. Journal of the American Dietetic Association, Vol. 25, pp. 39, January, 1949.

Directions and Literature from Equipment Companies.

Longree, Karla. Discoloration of Machine Peeled Potatoes. Journal of the American Dietetic Association. Vol. 32, pp. 639, July 1956.

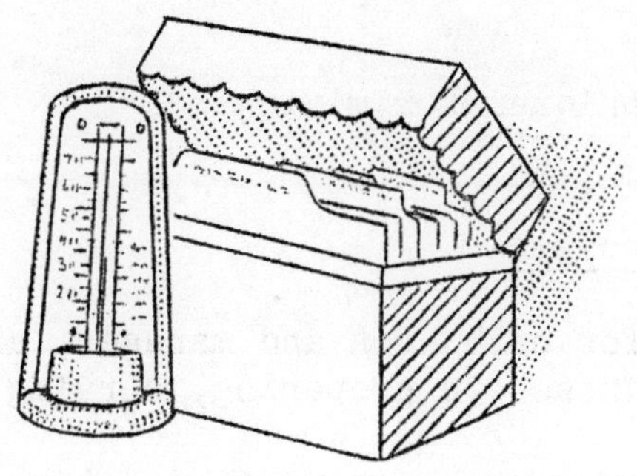

Chapter V

STANDARDIZATION-RECIPES AND PORTIONS

Cooking is an art and the cook is the artist. It is possible in quantity cookery to preserve both the art and artistry of preparation. Standardization does not eliminate the use of intelligent artistry and skill on the part of the worker and need not take away the individual touch and interest. In order to achieve quality products consistently methods, equipment, purchasing procedures, recipes and portions must be standardized. In previous chapters, we have discussed the first four. This chapter will be devoted to standardized recipes and portions.

STANDARD RECIPES

It is desirable for each food service unit to establish its own file of standard recipes. No manager can do an efficient job with scattered and untested recipes. Selected recipes may be in books, on separate sheets, or on cards. After recipes are tested and standardized, a card index is most practical as it permits more flexibility in filing. A 4" x 6" card is suggested. The system should usually follow the menu pattern of the establishment, and the recipes should be kept in a box to fit the size of card. A coat of white shellac will prolong the use of the card which can be wiped off when it becomes soiled. It is advisable to have a duplicate or master file. One set will be available for use by the manager and one for the staff. Any changes should be made on both sets. It is advisable to use basic recipes that have been carefully selected and tested. These can be varied sufficiently to give variety to the menu.

Before writing recipes all operations and equipment should be standardized.

1. Equipment and techniques for weighing

2. Size of pans in relation to yield

   Example:
   A 10" pie tin yields 8 servings.

3. Yields or size of servings

4. Serving equipment

5. Ingredients

6. Methods and techniques for mixing

Advantages of Standard Recipes

1. They save time for both cook and manager, allowing more time and money for skill and finesse in preparing, serving and merchandising of food.

2. They eliminate guesswork and waste due to poor estimating of quantities and failures in cooking.

3. They eliminate variations in quality and quantity of product, making frequent sampling and "doctoring" unnecessary.

4. They simplify the job of training a new worker.

5. They assist in food cost control by providing a means of:
   a. Figuring accurate cost of the material used.
   b. Estimating yield to be expected.
   c. Checking losses and making necessary adjustments by use of fewer or cheaper materials.
   d. Maintaining quality.
   e. Preventing leftovers.

Suggestions for Setting Up a Recipe File

1. Decide on the most practical form to use.

2. Decide on the desirable yield of recipes. Recipes for fifty or one hundred or the yields from modular size pans are recommended. Several multiples of the same recipe may be desirable, but each multiple should be on a separate card or on the reverse side in order to avoid mistakes.

3. Decide whether to use weights or measures or both. The usual procedure is to use measures for quantities under 25 and weights for those over 25. It is recommended that dry ingredients be weighed and that liquid ones be measured.

4. Express all quantities in usable figures. Avoid fractions. Convert all measures into the largest possible unit.

   Examples:
   a. Change 3/8 cup to ½ cup
   b. Change 4 cups to 1 quart
   [See Bibliography for conversion tables.]

5. Use the same abbreviations in all recipes. Be sure they are easy to read.

6. List all ingredients in the order used, and use correct terminology and any necessary qualifying statements.

   Examples:
   Baking powder, tartrate
   Cream, whipped or whipping

7. Give directions in detailed, concise and exact terms.
   a. Give mixingmethod, whether by hand or by machine and give exact time.
   b. Give size and kind of equipment to use for mixing and baking.
   c. List exact temperatures, cooking times or other necessary controls.
   d. Suggest variations of recipe.

8. Give directions for serving.

   Examples:
   a. Serving dish to use, size and kind
   b. Serving equipment-ladle or ounces
   c. Number and yield of servings expected
   d. Garnish or sauce

9. State cost of recipe. Check for seasonal changes in cost which might affect selling price.

10. Check and revise recipes periodically.
    a. For accuracy
    b. For improved and newer methods
    c. For time saving steps

11. Enrich your file by getting ideas for variations, garnishes or combinations from pictures, clippings and by dining out.

Sources of Recipes for a Quantity File

1. Available quantity recipes - these should be tested and adapted before adding to file.

2. Available small recipes - these will need to be tested and enlarged.

3. Basic recipes with suggestions for substitutions and variations

4. Recipes for prepared mixes

Procedures for Testing a Quantity Recipe

1. Select a basic recipe from a reliable source. Evaluate it as to proportions, methods, yield and cost to be sure the recipe is practical, suitable and scientifically sound.

2. Decide on any modifications necessary or desirable to make the recipe more suitable to your unit or to reduce cost.

3. Have a skilled worker make a recipe for 25 and judge the finished product. Make several tests if necessary.

4. Convert it to the desired yield for your establishment, if satisfactory. Check figures carefully, being sure all multiples are correctly stated and in usable terms. Convert into weights when possible.

5. Make the larger quantity and judge the quality of the finished product by using a standard rating scale and a carefully selected judging panel.

6. Run a popularity, cost, and yield study.

7. Have other units test and report results. If results are satisfactory, incorporate in your file.

Procedures for Enlarging Recipes

1. Evaluate the small recipe as to proportions, method, cost and yield. Decide whether it is correct, practical and suitable for your use.

2. Have a tester or skilled worker make twice the recipe and have result evaluated by a tasting panel. Run several tests, if necessary.

3. Enlarge the recipe for 50 or 100 servings. Make any necessary modifications or adjustments as to time, temperature or method. Convert amounts to weights when possible, and check figures for accuracy and usability. Check methods for clarity, conciseness and accuracy. Make any necessary modifications.

4. Have tester make the larger quantity and have results evaluated. Several tests may be necessary.

5. Have a regular cook make the enlarged recipe and have quality evaluated.

6. Run a popularity, cost and yield study.

7. Send out to other units and report results.

8. Incorporate in file, if satisfactory.

Use of Substitutes

The use of substitutes may be necessary because of shortages or emergencies; to reduce cost; as time-savers; to increase nutritive value or to utilize leftovers. A manager should become familiar with possible substitutes and their uses so that they can be incorporated in recipes quickly and accurately. The use of substitutes does not necessarily mean the use of cheap or inferior goods or the use of prepared or resale foods. A substitute should be equal in quality and food value to the original ingredient. The finished product can only be as good as the ingredients that go into it. The use of substitutes requires real skill, careful cooking techniques, good judgment and a real food sense. If directions are given by manufacturers, these directions should be followed carefully.

Procedure for Testing a Substitute

1. Run as many tests as needed to achieve a standard product.

2. Change only one ingredient at a time and use the same technique in each test.

3. Make a control product using the standard ingredients.

4. Compare and judge, using blind tests.

5. Judge final product for ease of preparation, quality, yield and cost.

Use of Prepared Mixes

Prepared mixes should be used only after they have been carefully checked for quality, food value, cost, and other factors. Ease of preparation should not be the only consideration.

Some prepared mixes may give a standard product but may be more expensive. However, the extra cost may be offset by the saving in labor and by fewer failures or variations of product due to carelessness of the workers. Each establishment will need to decide on the use of "mixes" in relation to its own problem.

Evaluating a Recipe

For all recipes tested, a testing committee or a tasting panel should be set up. The following points should be checked in evaluating a recipe.

1. Is the recipe clear, concise, accurate, and readable as to:
   a. Amounts in weights or measures
   b. Ingredients, type or kind
   c. Instructions for method
   d. Serving directions

      Examples:
      1. Size of serving
      2. Garnish to use

2. Does it produce a quality product as determined by score card?

3. Is the product nutritious?

4. Is it economical of time, energy and material?

5. Does it eliminate as far as possible the factor of human error?

6. Is the recipe suited to
   a. Clientele
   b. To available equipment
   c. To workers
   d. To type of service

7. Is the per capita cost of the product in line with the selling price?

Suggested Short Studies on Standard Recipes

1. File recipe cards according to menu chart. Study various ways of protecting recipes while in use, and apply method to your file.

2. Convert a recipe from measure to weight, and check for accuracy and time.

3. Have a class weigh and measure ingredients in a recipe, and check final results for accuracy and time.

4. Select a recipe and analyze it for usability.

5. Make or have available a numerical rating scale for a standard product of each food tested.

6. Run a test on volume and time for beating a mixture by hand versus machine.

7. Run a test on time for heating a volume of liquid in a double boiler on top of stove; in trunnion kettle, and in steamer. Suggest other studies where time in relation to volume is a factor in quantity work.

8. Cost several recipes, outlining all steps.

STANDARD PORTIONS

Lack of standard portions for serving is one of the greatest factors in the variation of profits in selling food. The food service manager should determine a suitable size of portion for each item served. Work sheets should carry necessary instructions regarding size and number of containers or pans to be used and size and number of portions to obtained. Suitable checks should be made to see that these yields are obtained. Even a few servings thrown away or not accounted for can make a sizeable difference in the actual cost of a food item.

The size of portion will depend on the age and activity of the group to be fed, the type of menu and service, and the profits expected. While standard servings are necessary, care should be taken not to have the plates look too standardized. Skill, variety of method, and artistry can overcome this danger. The use of portion control:

1. Makes possible the purchasing of the right amount of foods for the group to be fed and thus prevents over purchasing.

2. Prevents waste and loss of nutritive value due to reworking of left-overs.

3. Makes possible the use of fresh foods daily.

4. Assures standard yields from standard recipes and standard purchase units and thus prevents under or over production.

5. Assures ease in preparation and acceleration of food service.

6. Assures the minimum plate waste due to uneven portions.

7. Assures satisfaction of patrons by providing attractive and uniform servings.

8. Makes it possible to determine a proper selling price in relation to raw food cost.

9. Makes possible an accurate cost control system.

Suggestions for Standardizing Portions

1. Make use of standard guides.
   a. Charts showing exact yield for foods as purchased by specifications.
   b. Portion tables showing size of portion of foods as served in your unit.
   c. Standard recipes giving exact size of serving, count or weight.
   d. Control by count and tabulation studies indicating amount produced and actual number of servings obtained and sold. This assures careful cordination between kitchen and serving units.
   e. Multicounters or other machines to check portions served.
   f. Plate checks.

2. Train Workers
   a. In preparation techniques that will insure a standard product and a standard yield.
   b. In size of portion to be served and how to obtain these portions. The server should be trained to recognize the standard portion of each dish.

3. Provide Pre-portioning Tools and Equipment
   a. Standard-size pans that will permit portions to be cut or served as directed.

      Examples:
      Muffin tins
      Standard-size cake pans
      Meat loaf pans

   b. Standard and suitable ladles, spoons, dippers, ice cream dippers, tongs, of various sizes
   c. Individual casseroles, custard cups, molds, souffle cups
   d. Scales for weighed portions
   e. Slicers for breads, meats, or vegetables
   f. Cutters for butter, cheese, eggs, cakes, and pies
   g. Individual size milk bottles
   h. Individual cereal boxes
   i. Special envelopes containing portions of crackers, sugar, etc
   j. Individual cream pitchers

Suggested Short Problems on Standardized Portions

1. Make a list of foods that can be pre-portioned by:

a.	Slice	e.	Cuts
b.	Count	f.	Weight
c.	Measure	g.	Specification
d.	Dish or container	h.	Others

2. Work out the quantity necessary to serve various menus to 200 people.

3. Check plates for quantity served. Note possible reasons for the variation.

4. Make a study of plate returns, and check the relationship to serving techniques.

5. Make a study of the use of leftovers. Discuss ways in which leftovers could have been avoided.

Long Problems on Standard Recipes

1. Examine various standard quantity-recipe files or books for readability, content, and usability. Make a complete bibliography of quantity recipe books, citing special features of each.
   a. Give reasons for weights and measures used in various recipes.
   b. List reliable commercial sources of tested quantity recipes.
   c. List reliable sources of small-quantity recipes that could be enlarged.
   d. Cite a recipe with poor directions that would cause failure.

2. Incorporate one or more recipes in your file involving:
   a. Testing
   b. Enlarging recipe
   c. Substituting an ingredient
   d. Varying a basic recipe or food

3. Compile and adapt to quantity use tables that will help in analyzing all aspects of a recipe to be tested, such as variation of ingredients when enlarging a recipe, substituting ingredients or changing timing or temperature.

4. List methods you would use:
   a. To train and motivate cooks to use standard recipes where they have not been used to doing so.
   b. To introduce a new recipe in your kitchen or in a chain.
   c. To be sure recipes were followed as given.

5. Compile the following tables that would be helpful in testing recipes:
   a. Conversion
   b. Modification
   c. Substitution
   d. Judging

6. Give detailed instruction and equipment for measuring and weighing.

7. Make a study of variations of standard recipes.

8. Suggest others.

Long Problems on Standard Portions

1. Compile or check various yield charts for foods as purchased and prepared.

2. Compile or check various portion tables for foods served in various units on campus. Discuss variation.

3. Set up a demonstration and training program for workers in the use of standard portion devices. Show difference in results after training period.

4. Suggest others.

TABULATION STUDIES

A tabulation study is a detailed check on the amount of food purchased, prepared or cooked and the number of servings obtained. Poor planning, lack of coordination between units and poor instruction of workers may result in considerable loss. Frequent tabulation studies by management:

1. Provide a check on yield from various grades or units purchased.

2. Control costs by providing data on the cost of foods on the menu.

3. Aid in purchasing by showing discrepancies between food bought, prepared, and actually sold.

4. Prevent poor menu-making by showing the relative popularity of dishes prepared.

5. Provide a guide to amount to prepare.

6. Control production by preventing over or underproduction.

7. Control service by giving an accurate check on portions expected.

8. Give a check on any losses.

<u>Suggestions for Making a Tabulation Study</u>

1. Prepare or obtain a data sheet for information to be obtained.

2. Decide what specific dishes on menu are to be studied.

3. List them on tabulation sheet.

4. Get the following data for each food to be studied:
    a. Amount ordered and received
    b. Actual volume, weight, or count of food prepared
    c. Yield expected in volume and portions
    d. Portion measure

5. Give instructions to servers, and check to see how they are followed.

6. Set up a checking device to determine exact number of portions obtained and sold.

7. Check volume and servings left over.

8. Summarize and discuss:
    a. Spread between anticipated and actual yield and possible ways to correct.
    b. Spread between amount planned and leftovers and ways to correct.
    c. Per capita serving cost of food actually sold.

Date ____________________

TABULATION CHART

Name ____________________

Food item	Amount prepared			Total cost	Est. No. of servings	Servings obtained	Amount leftover	Real cost per serving	Selling price	Remarks
	A.P. Wt.	E.P. Wt.	% Waste							Explain variation, why leftovers, how to use leftovers, etc.
<u>Meat</u>										
1.										
2.										
<u>Èntree</u>										
1.										
2.										
<u>Vegetable</u>										
1.										
2.										
<u>Potatoes</u>										
1.										
2.										
<u>Salad</u>										
1.										
2.										
<u>Dessert</u>										
1.										
2.										

TABULATION CHART

Date ____________ Name ____________

Food item	Amount prepared: A.P. Wt.	Amount prepared: E.P. Wt.	Amount prepared: % Waste	Total cost	Est. No. of servings	Servings obtained	Amount leftover	Real cost per serving	Selling price	Remarks: Explain variation, why leftovers, how to use leftovers, etc.
Meat										
1.										
2.										
Entree										
1.										
2.										
Vegetable										
1.										
2.										
Potatoes										
1.										
2.										
Salad										
1.										
2.										
Dessert										
1.										
2.										

TABULATION CHART

Date ____________ Name ____________

Food item	Amount prepared			Total cost	Est. No. of servings	Servings obtained	Amount leftover	Real cost per serving	Selling price	Remarks
	A.P. Wt.	E.P. Wt.	% Waste							Explain variation, why leftovers, how to use leftovers, etc.
<u>Meat</u>										
1.										
2.										
<u>Entree</u>										
1.										
2.										
<u>Vegetable</u>										
1.										
2.										
<u>Potatoes</u>										
1.										
2.										
<u>Salad</u>										
1.										
2.										
<u>Dessert</u>										
1.										
2.										

Suggested Short Studies on Tabulation

1. Using the following chart make a tabulation study on several vegetables to determine relative yield, popularity and plate waste. Explain reasons for leftovers, if any.

2. Study cost of pre-portioned meats versus carved meats.

3. Work out relative efficiency of different counting or checking devices.

4. Explain ways of securing better coordination between the production and serving units.

5. Make a popularity study of various foods or "specials" expressed in percentage of number of people served.

6. Suggest other studies.

BIBLIOGRAPHY

Standardized Recipes

Fowler, Sina and Bessie Brooks West. Food for Fifty. New York: John Wiley and Sons.

Hart, Constance. Recipes at Moderate Cost. New York: Croft and Sons Publishing Company.

Smith, E. Evelyn. Quantity Recipes for Quality Food. Minneapolis: Burgess Publishing Company.

Treat, Nola and Lenore Richards. Quantity Cookery. Boston: Little, Brown and Company.

Terrell, Margaret. Large Quantity Recipes. Philadelphia: J. B. Lippincott Company.

Sullivan, Lenora. Iowa State College Quantity Recipe File. Ames, Iowa: College Press.

War Department Recipes. Washington, D.C.: United States Government Printing Office.

The Cook Book of the United States Navy. Washington, D.C.: United States Government Printing Office.

Lowe, Belle. Experimental Cookery. New York: John Wiley and Sons.

Minnesota Food Score Cards. Princeton, New Jersey: Cooperative Test Division. Education Test Service.

Harris, Katharine and Marion A. Wood. Quantity Recipes. Ithaca, New York: New York State College of Home Economics.

American Home Economics Association. Handbook of Food Preparation. 1954.

Casteen, Marie. Tested Recipes for Better Food. Journal of Home Economics, Vol. 30, pp. 559. October, 1938.

Barber, Mary and Katherine Gordon. Recipe Writing and Arithmetic. Journal of the American Dietetic Association, Vol. 15, pp. 273. April, 1939.

Dodge, Quindara. Menu Planning and Food Cost Control. Journal of the American Dietetic Association, Vol. 16, pp. 882. November, 1940.

Nettleton, Bertha. Food Control Through Recipes. Journal of the American Dietetic Association, Vol. 17, pp. 24. January, 1941.

Eliason, Winifred. Emergency Economics. Journal of the American Dietetic Association, Vol. 18, pp. 836. December, 1942.

Lund, Jeanette, and Mary E. Lyons. Substitution of Georgia Cane Syrup for Sucrose in Cakes. Journal of the American Dietetic Association, Vol. 19, pp. 492. July, 1943.

Wilmot, Jennie S. Substitutes, Extender, Deceivers. Journal of the American Dietetic Association, Vol. 19, pp. 505. July, 1943.

Melnick, Daniel; Richard J. Block, Hillard Himes and Bernard Oser. A comparative Analytical Study of Meat Extension. Journal of the American Dietetic Association, Vol. 20, pp. 150. March, 1944.

Williams, Stella. Standardization of Food and Recipes at Hardings. Journal of the American Dietetic Association, Vol. 22, pp. 144. February, 1946.

Smith, Erma. Use of Standardized Recipe Cards and Filing Systems. Journal of the American Dietetic Association, Vol. 22, pp. 1098. December, 1946.

Atkinson, Alta. Good Taste in Food Starts with a Standard Recipe File. Hospitals. May, 1948.

Kirkpatrick, Marie and Gertrude Sunderlin. The Master Mix in Quantity. Journal of the American Dietetic Association, Vol. 25, pp. 54. Januray, 1949.

Janssen, Pearl Z. Evaluation and Simplification of Recipes. Journal of the American Dietetic Association, Vol. 28, pp. 425. May, 1952.

Knickrehm, Marie. Formula and Methods for Preparing a Cake Mix in Quantity. Journal of the American Dietetic Association, Vol. 28, pp. 723. August, 1952.

Janssen, Pearl Z. Recipe Construction, Journal of the American Dietetic Association, Vol. 29, pp. 125. Feb., 1953.

Aldrich, Pearl. Scaling Home Recipes for Institutional Use. Kitchen Reporter, Kelvinator. January, 1943. Journal of the American Dietetic Association, Vol. 29, pp. 366. April , 1953, (abstract).

Kelley, Jeanette. Raising Food Standards Through Consumer Recipe Testing. Journal of the American Dietetic Association, Vol. 29, pp. 579. June, 1953.

Vail, Gladys E. Food Technology Solves Your Problems. Journal of the American Dietetic Association. Vol. 32, pp. 13, Jan. 1956.

Roller, Monica. Comparison of Products Made From Commercial Mixes and Conventional Formulas. Journal of the American Dietetic Association. Vol. 32, pp. 654, July 1956.

Hefner, Larne. Quality and Cost of Conventional vs. Premix Cakes. Journal of the American Dietetic Association. Vol. 33, pp. 233, March 1957.

BIBLIOGRAPHY ON STANDARD PORTIONS

Harris, Katherine and Marian Wood. Quantity Recipes from Meals for Many. New York State College of Home Economics, Cornell University, Ithaca, New York.

Fowler, Sina and Bessie Brooks West. Food for Fifty. New York: John Wiley and Sons.

Dunning, Frances. Cafeteria Service. Minneapolis: Burgess Publishing Company.

Dahl, J. O. Food Standard Handbook for Quantity Cookery. Stanford, Conn. Gold Book Series.

Byrnes, Margaret. Portion Control. Journal of the American Dietetic Association, Vol. 17, pp. 249. March, 1941.

Wenzel, George L. Cutting Costs Through Portion Control. American Restaurant, September, 1946.

Wenzel, George L. Portion control Mathematics. American Restaurant, August, 1947.

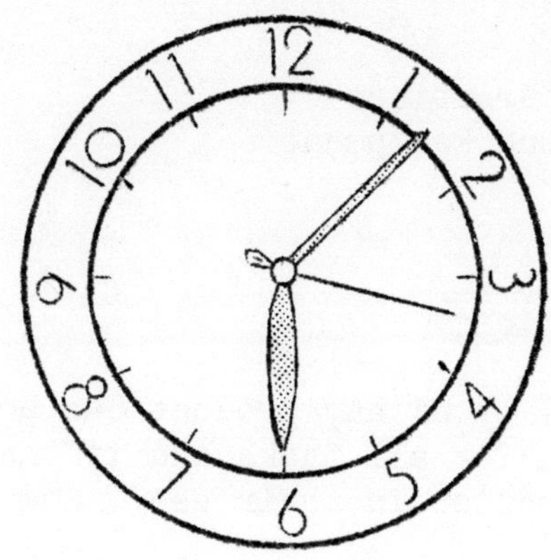

Chapter VI

WORK SIMPLIFICATION

Work simplification is the study of tasks and operations or a group of operations to determine the most efficient method of performance. Such studies cut down on the drudgery and routine of jobs, thus allowing more time for skill and joy in the final assembly of the finished product. Industry has used work simplification techniques for some time, and many of these can and need to be adapted to food service units if they are to compete with industry on the labor market.

Principles, techniques, implementation and data must be worked out to guide food managers in the wise use of employees' time. The aim is not necessarily to produce more in a given time, but to produce more efficiently with less fatigue to the workers. Worker's fatigue is always expensive to management as it causes deterioration of quality, spoilage, and accidents. It also causes lowered capacity for work and a longer rest period is necessary for recuperation.

Three Steps in a Work Simplification Program Are:

1. MAKE READY
   Arrange or preposition correctly, all tools and supplies.

2. DO
   Use correct standard procedures in proper sequence. Omit any unnecessary steps or duplication of steps. Use correct hand, arm and body motions.

3. PUT AWAY
   Carry through to completion all operations started. Clean up and put away.

STANDARDIZATION OF WORK TECHNIQUES

For a successful work simplification program, standardization of work techniques is essential in order to obtain data on how much of any task can be accomplished in a given time and the cost of an hour's work in relation to output. Thus, the cost of like jobs could be established in any locality. Standardization of work technique involves the use of:

Standard Methods and Practices
Standard Work Space and Equipment
Standard Motions

Standard Methods and Practices

Variables in the quality of any product can be avoided if standard methods and practices are employed for all tasks and if the worker is given the necessary directions and instruction in their use. Some suggestions for this standardization follow:

1. Make a plan and organize the work to be done.

2. Use the correct method and the proper sequence of operations.

3. Have a regular time for the doing of all jobs.

4. Collect all the proper equipment and preposition it around the workspace.

5. Collect and prepare all ingredients in order of assembly, thus using the fewest motions.

6. Dovetail all operations, performing all like operations at one time.

7. Provide for short rest periods or a change of job or position at the point where fatigue sets in. On long and repetitious jobs, there is a "warming up" period to a peak of optimum production which decreases as fatigue sets in. This repetitious optimum should be determined for all tasks.

Standard Work Space and Equipment

A worker should be provided with sufficient and well planned work space and correct tools and equipment if he is to accomplish standard results in the shortest time. There should be provided:

1. A functional floor plan with proper equipment, well selected and efficiently placed.

2. Comfortable work units
   a. Adequate and proper lighting and ventilation
   b. Sound deadening
   c. Clean, sanitary and safe work units

3. A well planned workspace
   a. Adequate space to allow for prepositioning of materials, tools and equipment within easy reach of the worker and as near the body as possible. A curved work space requires less stretching.
   b. Material and tools arranged in sequence of motions. Work should proceed in proper sequence and from right to left and should allow for the use of the assembly line system for long processes.

4. Suitable Equipment
   a. Proper work height for tables.
   b. Proper type, height and position of chairs to be used at work tables. A foot stool should be provided under tables. The worker should alternate between standing and sitting on long process jobs.
   c. Proper devices to free hands from holding and from manual work.

      Examples:
      Vices, machinery, fixtures, belts, foot pedals, gravity food bins, feed slides, drop deliveries and carts

   d. Combination tools

      Example:
      Perforated spoons

   e. Equipment providing proper leverage

      Example:
      Knives with long handles

   f. Properly placed levers, hand wheels and bars so that operator can manipulate them with least change in position.
   g. Well selected labor-saving devices and small equipment in good repair.

      Examples:
      Wheel carts and dollies
      Trays for collecting ingredients
      Scissors
      Proper size and shape of knives for work to be done
      Rubber scrapers for cleaning bowls
      Vegetable brushes
      Ice cream dippers for portioning
      Standard size pans
      Scales
      Large measuring containers
      Thermometers
      Clocks and timers

Standard Motions

A worker should be able to accomplish his work with the least fatigue possible. He can best do this if he follows some of the suggested body, hand and finger motions.

1. Avoid unnecessary reaching, stretching, and bending.
2. Use both hands, when possible, starting and completing motions at the same time.

   Example:
   Putting plates on tray

3. Form habits by continual use of correct motions.

4. Move arms in opposite and symmetrical directions and simultaneously, rather than in the same direction.

5. Use simple, balanced continuous and rhythmic hand motions.

6. Distribute hand and body motions.
   a. Finger motion
   b. Finger and wrist
   c. Finger, wrist and lower arm
   d. Finger, wrist and upper arm
   e. Finger, wrist, arms and body

7. Make use of momentum, acceleration and gravity to accomplish tasks.

8. Avoid sudden sharp stops.

9. Use curved rather than straight line motions involving sudden and sharp changes in direction, especially on long processes.

Suggestions for Work Simplification in Various Kitchen Units

Management

Menu pattern
Simplified menus
Menu chart
Standard recipe file
Basic recipes with variations
Standard forms for requisitions, records, etc.
Good filing systems
Schedule for buying
Counting devices, charts, graphs, etc.
Up-to-date library of helpful books
Schedules
Definite directions for workers
Detailed work schedules for new workers

Range Unit

1. Keep a mix of flour and fat in refrigerator (a roux). Make all white sauce needed at one time.

2. Use a wire whip for mixing flour and water for gravies and sauces.

3. Put a little oil on top of water to prevent starchy foods from boiling over.

4. Keep bulk foods on hand.

   Examples:
   Cocoa paste
   Syrups

5. Use cooking containers for serving when possible.

   Example:
   Casseroles

6. Grind several foods in succession when possible to save time in washing grinder. Grind some dry bread to help clean machine.

7. Keep bread crumbs on hand.

8. Make croquette mixtures a day ahead and chill.

9. Weigh all portions.

10. Oven-fry chops and bacon when possible to save time and handling.

Vegetable Unit

1. Use all techniques of time and motion previously discussed.

2. Use vegetable brushes for cleaning vegetables.

3. Use correct knives for peeling and dicing and make use of boards,

4. Hold a cluster of beans or strips of carrots in hand and cut crosswise on a board with one pull of knife.

5. Peel onions under water or cut in quarters and slip skins off.

6. Cut large stems off spinach or broccoli to save cooking time. These may be cooked separately.

7. Pick over and wash parsley and store in covered jar.

8. Use wedges or whole vegetables when practical.

9. Avoid peeling potatoes when possible.

10. Use all machines and labor-saving devices to standardize size of serving portions.

Salad Unit

1. Note short cuts as listed under vegetable unit.

2. Trim lettuce and place in polyethelene bags in refrigerator.

3. Core a head of lettuce and allow water to run through the head to separate leaves for lettuce cups.

4. Use assembly line system for salad assembly. Make use of both hands and perform all of one operation at a time. See Chart I.

5. Keep supply of all salad dressings on hand.

6. Peel and section grapefruit and oranges over a bowl.

7. Drain all salad ingredients, especially canned fruits and vegetables, to prevent leaking.

8. Use labor-saving devices and equipment to allow time for attractive arrangements.

9. Use a knife wrapped with oil paper to separate butter cubes.

10. Make use of carts and dollies for transporting ingredients and finished salads.

Pastry Unit

1. Weigh rather than measure.

2. Use largest size equipment for weighing or measuring.

   Examples:
   Quarts or gallon measures

3. Collect all ingredients and preposition them.

4. Sift flour directly into measure.

5. Roll sticky foods in powdered sugar before chopping.

6. Thicken juice of berries or fruits before adding filling to pies.

7. Chill cream, bowl and beater before whipping cream.

8. Heat only enough liquid to dissolve gelatin when making gelatin salads or desserts.

9. Weigh or measure batter into pans to assure even volume. Dropping pan on table after filling will level mixture.

10. Frost cake on sides first and finish on top.

11. Dip knife in hot water when cutting pies or cakes.

12. Cut and frost cakes on a tray or brown paper to facilitate cleaning up.

13. Avoid extra handling of doughs or batter, when practical.

    Examples:
    a. Drop cookies rather than rolled
    b. Ice box cookies

14. Cut down on pans in baking.

    Example:
    Use aluminum foil or individual paper cups.

15. Make up pastry crumbs (fat and flour) and keep on hand.

16. Portion by weighing pastry for pies and roll all crusts at one time. Stack by placing wax paper between. These may be kept overnight in refrigerator.

17. Use markers to obtain even cuts of pies and cakes.

18. Use master mixes when practical.

19. Keep a mixture of sugar and cinnamon and chopped nuts on hand.

20. Use thermometers and thermostats.

21. Use carts, racks or trays for transporting supplies and finished products.

10. Place pan of bread first, and finish on top.

16. Portion by weighing pastry for pies and refrigerate if one time use. Stack by placing wax paper between. These may be kept overnight for rolling out.

18. Use mechanical mixer when practical.

Suggestions for Demonstrations on Short Cuts

1. Use of proper knives for various purposes
2. Peeling of oranges and grapefruit
3. Sectioning of oranges and grapefruit
4. Coring and slicing of apples
5. Making lettuce cups
6. Scraping of carrots
7. Cutting carrots and beans in strips
8. Mincing, dicing, chopping of meat, vegetables or fruits using a French knife
9. Slicing tomatoes, green peppers
10. Assembly line salad set-up
11. Egging and crumbing of pork chops
12. Put on a demonstration of making and wrapping sandwiches in quantity using work simplification technique.

Chart I

EXAMPLE OF ASSEMBLY LINE SYSTEM

SALAD MAKING

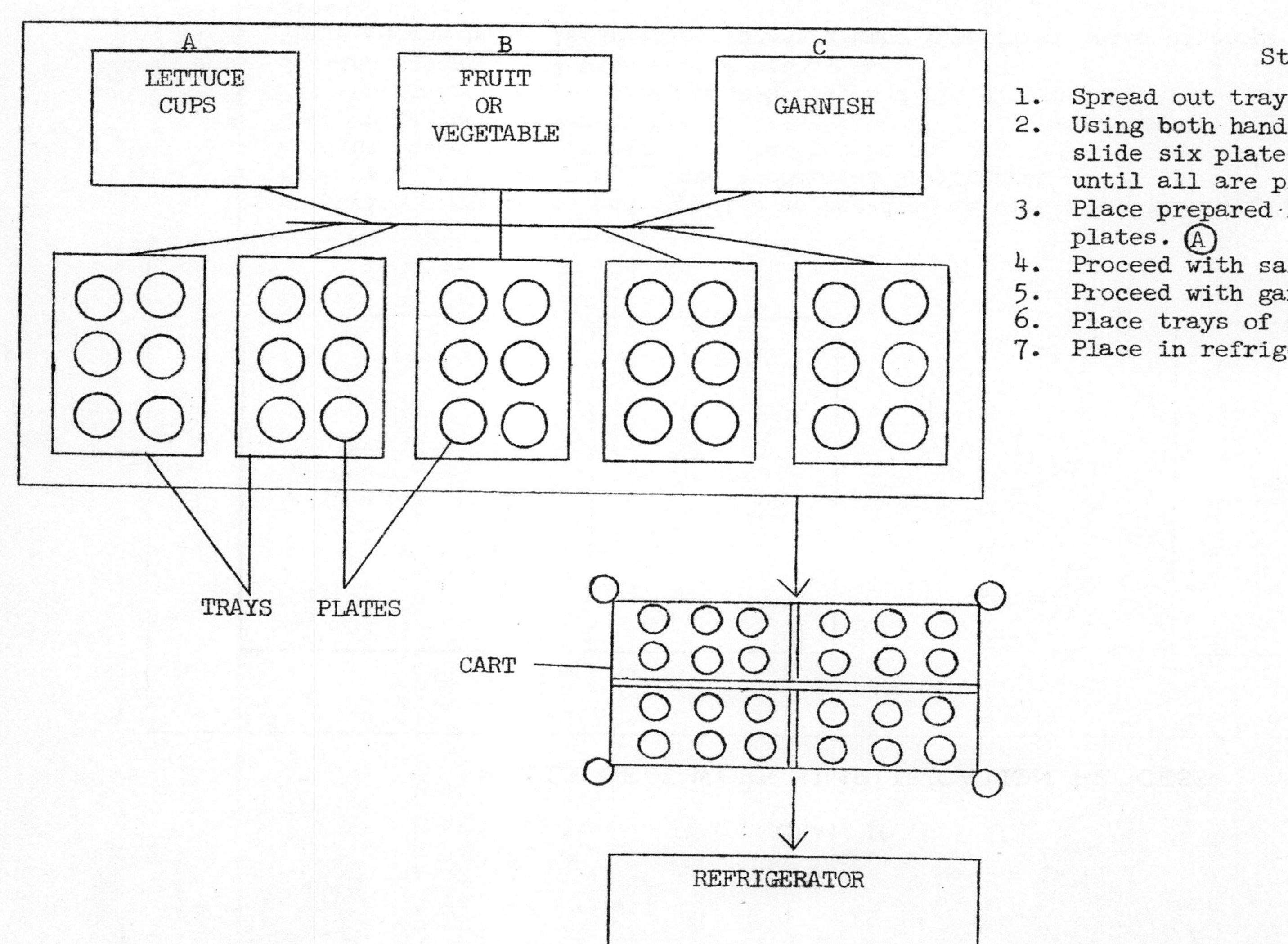

Steps

1. Spread out trays.
2. Using both hands and drop motion, slide six plates on tray. Continue until all are placed.
3. Place prepared lettuce cups on all plates. (A)
4. Proceed with salad ingredients. (B)
5. Proceed with garnish. (C)
6. Place trays of salads on carts.
7. Place in refrigerator.

Chart II

SAMPLE OF A WORK SIMPLIFICATION PROCESS

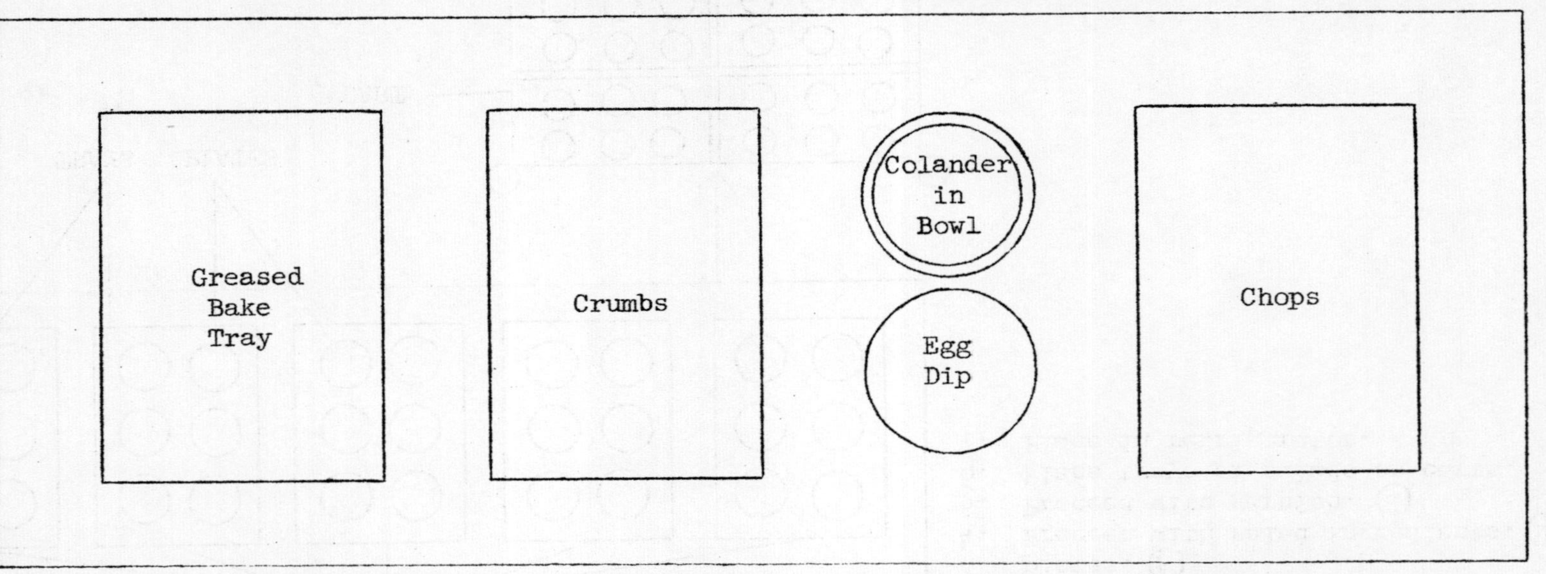

1. Preposition equipment and supplies as per diagram with right to left flow.
2. Pick up <u>four</u> chops in <u>each</u> hand, separated by fingers.
3. Holding these chops in each hand emmerse in the egg.
4. Drop chops in colander to drain.
5. Pick up drained chops, using both hands, and place in crumbs.
6. Continue steps 2 - 3 with second batch.
7. While second batch is draining, press crumbs into first batch of chops - turn over - press on the crumbs.
8. Place on greased bake sheet. Turn over to grease on both sides.
9. Continue with rest of chops.
10. Bake at 450-500° F.

Suggested Short Studies on Work Simplification

1. Make a study of fatigue on repetitious jobs.

2. Make a complete time and motion study in each work unit:
   a. Reduce present practice to writing.
   b. Enumerate motions used.
   c. Eliminate variables which affect motion.
   d. Reduce best practice to writing.
   e. Repeat to form correct habits.

3. Determine the hourly labor cost in relation to output on such jobs as:
   a. Making salads
   b. Eyeing potatoes
   c. Cutting butter

4. Make an hourly work curve to determine fatigue of workers. Replan schedules with results of this study in mind.

5. Note "Hints on Work Simplifications" for each unit. Add to this list.

6. Make a study of right to left and left to right operations and check for efficiency.

Suggested Long Studies on Work Simplification

1. Study the efficiency of a worker at various hours of day and on various days of week. Make a work pattern based on the findings.

2. Set up and give a complete demonstration illustrating short cuts in methods, equipment and motion.

   Examples:
   a. Sandwich making
   b. Making and arranging salads.

3. Work out a complete demonstration of the types of body and hand motions that make for work simplification.

4. Make a study of the work efficiency of any worker. Retrain the worker in more efficient methods.

5. Compare work simplification techniques, equipment and efficiency of motion of workers in various types of institutions.

6. Compare work simplification habits of workers of various ages and experiences.

7. Apply your study of floor plans and equipment to a work simplification program.

8. Set up a training program for work simplification for a group of workers.

9. Make a study of the "master mix" as a time saver.

10. Make studies of prepared mixes as time savers in relation quality.

BIBLIOGRAPHY

Work Simplification

West, Bessie Brooks and LeVelle Wood. Food Service in Institutions. New York; John Wiley and Sons.

Schmid, Merle. Work Simplification in Hospitals. Industrial Management Engineers, 111 West Jackson Blvd. Chicago 4, Illinois.

Baines, Ralph. Motion and Time Study. New York: John Wiley and Sons.

Ryan, A. H. Fatigue Studies in Household tasks. Journal of Home Economics, Vol. 20, pp. 637-643. September, 1928.

Hess, Alfred. Efficiency in Motion. Journal of the American Dietetic Association, Vol. 17, pp. 438. May, 1941.

Stoddard, Charles. Time and Motion Studies for Labor Saving. American Restaurant, October, 1942.

Binns, Gertrude. Saving Time and Energy in Food Production and Service. Journal of the American Dietetic Association, Vol. 18, pp. 834. December, 1942.

Kearney, P. W. It pays to be Lazy. Journal of Home Economics, Vol. 36, pp. 237. April, 1944.

Gross, Irma. Research in Work Simplification. Journal of Home Economics, Vol. 37, pp. 159. March, 1945.

Schmid, Merle. Taking the Work out of Work. American Hospital Association Report, pp. 127-146. December, 1946.

Spickler, Joseph. Work Simplification as a Tool of Management. Journal of the American Dietetic Association, Vol. 24, pp. 598. July, 1948.

Welch, Frances, Reueline Hibler, Billie Sims and Jeanette Wright. Relation of Method to the Time Required for Preparing Vegetables. Journal of the American Dietetic Association, Vol. 24, pp. 690. August, 1948.

Schmid, Merle. Work Simplification-Making the Job Easier. Journal of the American Dietetic Association, Vol. 24, pp. 1062. December, 1948.

Kirkpatrick, M. Controlling Labor Cost. Restaurant Management, January, February, March, 1949.

Thomas, Orpha. Bringing Engineering Principles into Hospital Kitchens. Hospitals. August, 1949.

Stewart, Dorothy. Dietetic Interns Save Time. Journal of the American Dietetic Association, Vol. 26, pp. 804. October, 1950.

Rosa, Ercali. Work Simplification-A Tool in Reducing Food Costs. Journal of the American Dietetic Association, Vol. 27, pp. 952-956. November, 1951.

Blaker, Gertrude and Katherine Harris. Labor Hours and Labor Costs in a College Cafeteria. Journal of the American Dietetic Association, Vol. 28, pp. 429. May, 1952.

Frazer, J. Ronald. Methods Analysis. Journal of the American Dietetic Association, Vol. 29, pp. 786. August, 1953.

Wright, Marion. Work Simplification in the Dietary Department. Journal of the American Dietetic Association, Vol. 29, pp. 790. August, 1953.

Harrington, Mary. Work Simplification at Work. Journal of the American Dietetic Association, Vol. 29, pp. 779. August, 1953.

Carlson, John G. Planning Easier Work. Journal of the American Dietetic Association. Vol. 30, pp. 133, Feb. 1954.

Tuthill, Byrdine and Donaldson, Beatrice. Labor in the Dietary Department. Journal of the American Dietetic Association. Vol. 32, pp. 541, June 1956.

Mundel, M. E. Motion Study in Food Service. Journal of the American Dietetic Association. Vol. 32, pp. 546, June 1956.

Kotschevar, Lendal. One-Motion Storage. Institutions Magazine. Dec. 1956.

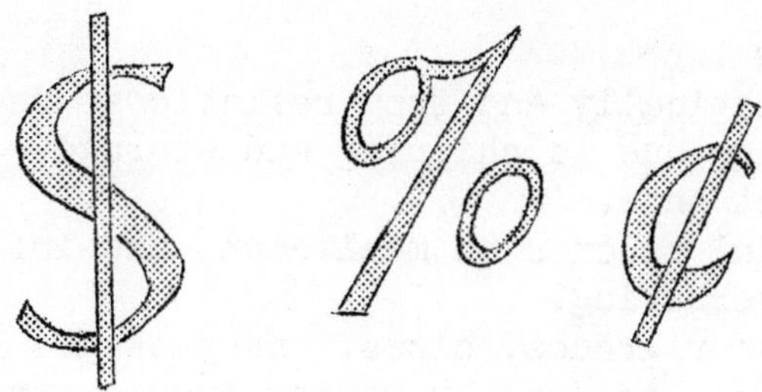

Chapter VII

CONSERVATION AND WASTE CONTROL

The food that is wasted is the food that really costs the most in any food service unit. To the cost of the original raw food must be added the labor and overhead cost, without a corresponding return from food sales. Careful control systems should be set up by management to prevent all causes for waste of food, labor and fuel. Each institution should determine by careful studies, how much waste is legitimate.

Food waste in kitchen, serving room and dining room will fall into two main classifications:

1. Avoidable waste
2. Unavoidable waste

Avoidable Waste

This includes all foods or parts of food which should be edible but which, because of poor handling, preparation, cooking or serving are discarded.

Examples:
a. Losses in nutritive value
b. Undue shrinkage
c. Plate waste

Unavoidable Waste

A minimum of unavoidable waste is legitimate. It may include parings, kitchen waste, bones and fat. The problem of waste control involves every aspect of food management, and is really an index of the efficiency of management.

A review of management problems in relation to waste control follows:

A. Proper menu-making
   1. Avoid too great a variety of foods.
   2. Use a selective menu when possible.
   3. Study the likes and dislikes of patrons, and make frequent popularity and serving studies to see that food is suitable in amount, kind and cost.

4. Study past records of consumption and attendance to prevent overproduction and undue leftovers.

B. Careful Buying
1. Buy systematically and from reliable sources to prevent shrinkage and spoilage due to shipping and storage. Check quality and quantity at once.
2. Keep careful records on meal count and influencing factors to prevent overbuying.
3. Select proper grades, sizes, and packages in relation to use. This can only be done by making frequent yield studies.
4. Study real versus apparent costs.
5. Avoid overstocking or overbuying.

C. Careful Storage of all Foods and Leftovers
1. Sort carefully.
2. Store immediately at proper temperature and under proper conditions.
3. Store in suitable containers. Avoid putting warm food in deep kettles in the refrigerator.
4. Avoid holding food too long, thus preventing shrinkage, spoilage and loss of nutritive value.

D. Proper Preparation
1. To prevent loss of nutritive value:
   a. Use proper cooking methods.
   b. Use all cooking liquors.
   c. Avoid unnecessary peeling.
   d. Avoid undue exposure of peeled or shredded food to water or air.
2. To prevent loss due to failures:
   a. Use tested recipes to avoid failure.
   b. Use standard practices and equipment to assure uniform products, less waste, and greater yield.
   c. Avoid over production.
   d. Use proper cooking techniques to prevent undue shrinkage or failure.
   e. Have foods properly cleaned and trimmed and utilize all usable parts to prevent unnecessary waste.
   f. Avoid too early preparation or long standing of foods on range or steam table. Use staggered cookery when possible.
   g. Make careful yield studies.
   h. Clean out all mixing bowls carefully. When possible, serve food from cooking container or bake pans to prevent loss due to transfer.
   i. Avoid reheating foods before serving.
   j. Train workers and carefully supervise each operation.
   k. Make waste studies and inspect garbage cans periodically.

E. Proper Service
1. Use portion controls to assure standard servings and to avoid plate waste.
2. Use proper serving equipment to assure portion control.
3. Use good merchandising techniques to assure saleability of food.

4. Use frequent tabulation, serving and plate return studies to see what is being returned and why.
5. Carefully train and supervise workers.

F. Wise Use of Leftovers
1. Use leftovers promptly. Carefully inspect icebox and storerooms daily.
2. Avoid overworking of leftovers.
3. Use leftovers in varied and interesting ways.

G. Prevention of Leakages
1. Faulty equipment or carelessness--inspect equipment frequently.
2. Pilfering--use control system and locked storerooms.

H. Supervision and Training
1. Supervise each operation and employee.
2. Make frequent waste studies and garbage inspection.
3. Change and modify policies as indicated by results of studies.
4. Work out training programs on waste prevention for all employees.

Waste Studies

Using the following charts, it will be possible to find the reasons for losses and to make a careful study of all sources of both avoidable and unavoidable waste. Controls or policies should then be initiated to prevent these leaks that result in high food cost.

WASTE CHART STUDY

KITCHEN						DINING ROOM									
	AVOIDABLE WASTE		UNAVOIDABLE WASTE			PLATE WASTE									
Failures	Poor Methods of Preparation	Usable Leftovers	Preparation												
			Vegetable skins etc.	Bones	Gristle Fat, Scraps	Bread	Cores, Skins Bones	Meat & Fish	Milk-Coffee	Vegetables Potatoes	Cereal	Salad	Pudding, Pies Cakes	Butter	Other

WASTE CHART STUDY

KITCHEN						DINING ROOM										
	AVOIDABLE WASTE		UNAVOIDABLE WASTE			PLATE WASTE										
Failures	Poor Methods of Preparation	Usable Leftovers	Preparation													
			Vegetable skins etc.	Bones	Gristle Fat, Scraps	Bread	Cores, Skins Bones	Meat & Fish	Milk-Coffee	Vegetables Potatoes	Cereal	Salad	Pudding, Pies Cakes	Butter	Other	

WASTE CHART STUDY

KITCHEN						DINING ROOM									
	AVOIDABLE WASTE		UNAVOIDABLE WASTE			PLATE WASTE									
Failures	Poor Methods of Preparation	Usable Leftovers	Preparation												
			Vegetable skins etc.	Bones	Gristle Fat, Scraps	Bread	Cores, Skins Bones	Meat & Fish	Milk-Coffee	Vegetables Potatoes	Cereal	Salad	Pudding, Pies Cakes	Butter	Other

Suggested Studies on Waste

1. Make a chart showing amounts of waste that have been determined by various studies in the literature.

2. Outline and carry out a complete waste study in a food service unit.

3. Make a study of plate returns and outline suggested change in policies or management.

4. Study one food and note all waste, quantitative and qualitative, throughout all processes.

5. Make a study of "hidden leaks" and suggest ways of preventing them.

6. Use the chart to check all sources of waste in food production.

7. Make a comparative study of plate waste, using chart in various food service units on campus, and analyze results.

8. In each unit, make waste and shrinkage studies on typical foods prepared.

9. Suggest other studies.

BIBLIOGRAPHY ON WASTE

Nelson, Mable and Geneva Crouch. The Relation of the Quality of Vegetables to the Waste Incurred in Their Preparation. Journal of the American Dietetic Association, Vol. 9, pp. 107. July, 1933.

Whiteman, Elizabeth and Florance King. A Study of the Waste in Preparation and in Cooking of Fresh Vegetables. Journal of the American Dietetic Association, Vol. 14, pp. 615. October, 1938.

Harris, Zoe. Saving Food in Dormitory. Journal of the American Dietetic Association, Vol. 18, pp. 101. February, 1942.

Editorial. Methods of Checking and Evaluating Plate Waste. Journal of the American Dietetic Association, Vol. 20, pp. 376. June, 1944.

Oliver, Robert. Normal Food Wastage--A Socio-Economic Problem. American Scientist. Vol. 32, October, 1944.

Van Syckle, Calla. Some Pictures of Food Consumption in the United States. Journal of the American Dietetic Association, Part I. Vol. 21, pp. 508-512. September, October, 1945. Part II. Vol. 21, pp. 690-695. December, 1945.

Hageman, Mary Irene. A Study of Plate Waste as a Directive Measure in Food Conservation. Journal of the American Dietetic Association, Part I. Vol. 21, pp. 608. November, 1945. Part II. Vol. 21, pp. 685, December, 1945.

Mitchell, Margaret. Production Management in Today's Kitchen. Journal of the American Dietetic Association, Vol. 23, pp. 25. January, 1947.

Welch, Frances, et al. Food Waste in Relation to Weight as Purchased vs. Edible Portions Portions. Journal of the American Dietetic Association, Vol. 23, pp. 522. June, 1947.

Worden, Robert. How Scientifically Developed Food Purchasing Standards Cut Cost. Restaurant Management. pp. 49, June, 1948.

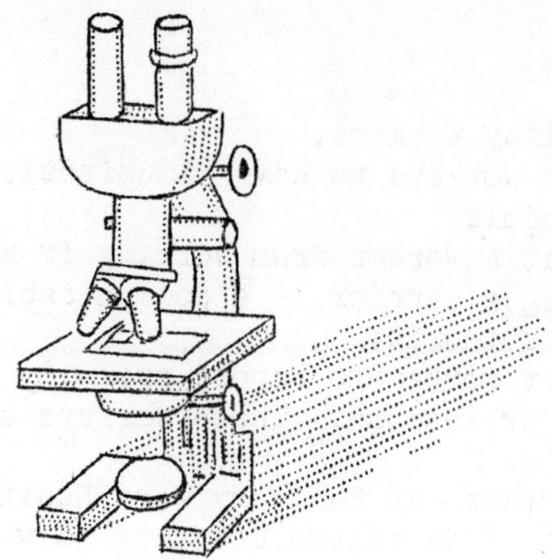

Chapter VIII

SANITATION TECHNIQUES AND ACCIDENT PREVENTION

GOOD FOOD IS SAFE FOOD - It is the responsibility of the manager and subsequently of the employees to insure the serving of safe food to the public. Every manager should obtain copies of the federal, state and local sanitary codes issued by the respective health departments, regulating eating and drinking establishments. The standards established by these codes must be enforced to insure protection of the public.

SANITATION STANDARDS

A. Purchase Safe Foods.
   1. Buy pasteurized fresh milk and milk products and store in refrigerator until served.
   2. Buy only inspected meats. The federal inspected meat bears a federal inspected stamp.
   3. Buy seafood from sources approved by the state health department or from dealers on U. S. Public Health list. Shucked shellfish should be bought in original packing container showing packer's state and certificate number.
   4. Avoid purchase of foods that have been exposed, e.g., unwrapped bread or pastry not kept in covered containers.
   5. Avoid use of home canned foods unless assured that safe methods were employed in their processing. Never use bulged cans or canned foods having an off-odor or mold.
   6. Buy frozen foods that have been kept frozen. Frozen foods should not be thawed and refrozen.

B. Store and Handle Foods Properly.
   1. Store supplies appropriately as soon as delivered.
   2. Store staple items in cans or jars with tight fitting covers.
   3. Store semi-perishables, e.g., potatoes, onions, citrus fruits, and apples in a cool room for short periods.
   4. Refrigerate meats, poultry, fish, eggs, dairy products, cooked foods such as cream pie fillings and opened canned foods below 40° F. These foods should be kept in covered containers.
   5. Store foods off the floor at all times.
   6. Cool foods quickly. Store foods in refrigerator in small shallow containers to assure complete cooling.

C. Employ Healthy Workers.
   1. Require workers to have immunization tests and periodic examinations if possible.
   2. Prohibit a worker from working if he is suspected of contraction or being a carrier of a communicable disease. Notify the nearest health authority.
   3. Instruct worker to report promptly colds or other illness, sores, wounds or lesions. These workers should not be allowed to work.

D. Instruct Workers in Sanitary Work Habits.
   1. To wash hands before starting to work and after using handerchief or toilet. Hand sinks with soap and paper towels should be available.
   2. To be well groomed, clean and neat. Clean washable outer garments, apron or coats should be worm when preparing or serving food. Hairnet, head bands or caps should be worn to confine hair.
   3. To use towels and service cloths properly. They should always be clean and used only for purposes intended. They should not be carried on employees' shoulder or arm.
   4. To handle dishes and utensils in a sanitary manner. Glasses and cups should be handled by the bases, and silver by the handles. A demonstration should be given worker on these techniques.
   5. To use a tasting spoon, not fingers for tasting.
   6. To avoid use of tobacco while on duty and never to expectorate where food is being prepared or served.

E. Plan Careful Housekeeping.
   1. Make a definite cleaning schedule which is frequently checked by supervisors for high standards of cleanliness and sanitation.
      a. Work surfaces and equipment (tables, meat blocks, stoves, sinks, peelers, mixers, cooking and eating utensils, etc.) should be thoroughly cleaned after each use.
      b. Refrigerators should be defrosted and thoroughly cleaned at regular and frequent intervals.
      c. Storerooms should be kept clean and orderly in arrangement.
      d. Leftovers and other food should not be exposed at any time. They should be stored immediately in covered containers.
      e. Garbage and other wastes should be removed daily. The containers used for garbage should be scalded and aired. They should be kept covered always between periods of use.
      f. Screens, insecticides and other effective measures must be employed for protection from dust, flies, rodents, roaches, and vermin.

F. Plan Safe Dishwashing.
   Detailed instructions for dishwashing must be given elsewhere but a review of basic procedures is pertinent here. A dishwashing machine and adequate dishwashing space should be provided. When possible the unit should work from right to left for efficiency.
   1. Machine Washing
      a. Remove all food particles from dishes using a rubber scraper.
      b. Prerinse dishes at 80° F. Wash at 130-140° F. and rinse at 170-180° F. Avoid toweling.
      c. Store dishes in clean, dry, closed cupboards. Invert cups and glasses.

2. Hand Washing
    a. Use a three compartment sink.
    b. Use a sanitizing agent such as chlorine.
    c. Do not towel.

G. Plan Safe Pot and Pan Washing
1. Use a three compartment sink.
2. Soak in warm water and scrape out loosened food.
3. Wash in clean, soapy, hot water. Use a pot washing brush and change water frequently. Detergent instead of soap may be employed.
4. Rinse in clean, hot chlorine solution and drain. Toweling is not necessary if rinse water is very hot.

Review Questions on Sanitation

1. A Good Sanitary Code

   Do you have one in your community?

2. Safe Source of Food--Properly Handled

   Do you buy inspected meat, pasteurized milk, safe water and no exposed food?

   Do you prevent food from standing at room temperature too long during preparation?

3. Proper Storage

   Is all food put in covered containers?

   Do you have a good refrigerator and maintain a temperature at about 40° F.?

4. Healthy Workers

   Are the workers free from colds or other communicable diseases?

5. Good Work Habits

   Do the workers wear hairnets and clean wash dresses while cooking?

   Do they refrain from using fingers for tasting?

   Do they handle dishes properly?

   Do they wash their hands before starting to work or after using a handkerchief?

6. Careful Housekeeping

   Do you have a regular schedule for care and cleaning of the kitchen? "Everybody's work is no one's." Do you have a score card for your unit?

7. Safe Dishwashing

   Is your dishwashing adequate, proper height, and routed from right to left?

   Do you wash dishes at 130° F. and rinse at 180° F.? If not, do you use a chlorine solution? Do you have a prerinse?

   Do you avoid toweling dishes?

   Do you store dishes in closed closets?

ACCIDENT PREVENTION

Accidents are expensive to the worker and to the management and every precaution should be taken to assure a safe work unit. A fire extinguisher, a fire blanket and a first aid kit should be placed where they can be easily reached and the worker should be instructed in their use. The following suggestions for accident prevention should be posted in all work units.

A. To avoid cuts
1. Store knives and other cutting tools in racks with blades protected.
2. Use sharp cutting tools of correct size and with the proper blade for work to be done.
3. Use a board for all cutting, dicing, mincing.
4. Cut downward, never toward hand.
5. Collect all sharp tools on tray and wash separately. Never leave them in dishwater.
6. Use mechanical peelers for paring fruits and vegetables when possible.
7. Discard broken dishes, defective utensils and opened tin cans. Handle these with care.

B. To Avoid Burns
1. Use pot holders to handle hot utensils. Do not use towels or aprons.
2. Do not reach into ovens. Use a puller or proper tool to bring the pans to front of oven before removing.
3. Follow carefully instructions for use of steamers, trunnions, and steam tables.
4. Avoid filling kettles too full.
5. Avoid spattering, splashing or allowing food to boil over.
6. Stir with long handled spoons.
7. Avoid fat fires. Do not fill fat containers too full. If fat should catch on fire, place a cover over it at once. Do not lift from stove. Salt may be placed on grease fire on stove.
8. Should a worker's clothes catch on fire,use the fire blanket immediately.
9. Allow steam table, oven and stove to cool before cleaning.

C. To Avoid Miscellaneous Accidents
1. Keep floors clean and dry to avoid slipping.
2. Have straight traffic lines, and "in and out" doors to avoid collisions.
3. Keep all traffic lines and exits and entrances clear.
4. Handle electric equipment with dry hands.
5. Check pilot lights and all burners before lighting gas.
6. Load and carry trays carefully. Do not tilt or overcrowd them.
7. Keep all closet doors closed.
8. Prohibit use of inflammable liquids.

BIBLIOGRAPHY

Sanitation

U.S. Public Health Code
State Public Health Code
Local Codes
Check Sheets

Troutt, Lute. Problems of Cleanliness in Food Handling. Journal of the American Dietetic Association, Vol. 10, pp. 24. May, 1934.

Fuller, James E. Some Public Health Aspects of Food. Journal of the American Dietetic Association, Vol. 14, pp. 412. June-July, 1938.

Harding, T. Swann. Poisons in Food, Fantasy or Fact. Journal of the American Dietetic Association, Vol. 14, pp. 436. June-July, 1938.

Atkinson, Alta. Safety Education. Journal of the American Dietetic Association, Vol. 17, pp. 248. March, 1941.

Tiedeman, Walter D. Public Health Aspects of Dishwashing. Journal of the American Dietetic Association, Vol. 17, pp. 546. June-July, 1941.

Tanner, Fred W. Sanitary Care and Handling of Food. Journal of the American Dietetic Association, Vol. 21, pp. 137. March, 1945.

Mallman, W. L. Sanitation of Institution Equipment. Journal of the American Dietetic Association, Vol. 21, pp. 142. March, 1945.

Mallman, W. L. Sanitation for Food Departments. Journal of the American Dietetic Association, Vol. 22, pp. 870. October, 1946.

Husseman, Dorothy L. and Fred W. Tanner. New Aspects of Food Poisoning Problem. Journal of the American Dietetic Association, Vol. 23, pp. 16. January, 1947.

Rice, Thurman B. Epidemiology of the Dining Table. Journal of the American Dietetic Association, Vol. 23, pp. 22. January, 1947.

Drayer, Joseph M. Methods of Employee Education in Sanitation. Journal of the American Dietetic Association, Vol. 23, pp. 884. October, 1947.

Kraybill, H. R. Protecting the Health of the Food Consumer. Journal of the American Dietetic Association, Vol. 24, pp. 17. Januray, 1948.

Francis, Kent W. Well-Managed Eating Places are Safe. Journal of the American Dietetic Association, Vol. 24, pp. 105. February, 1948.

Black, Lois and Martha Lewis. Effect on Bacteria Growth of Various Methods of Cooling Cooked Foods. Journal of the American Dietetic Association, Vol. 24, pp. 399-404. May, 1948.

National Research Council. Minimum Requirements for Effective Machine Dishwashing. Journal of the American Dietetic Association, Vol. 26, pp. 251. April, 1950.

McMahon, Grace. Dietary Consultant, A Service for Small Institutions. Journal of the American Dietetic Association, Vol. 26, pp. 958. December, 1950.

Buchanan, E. B. Dietary Consultant-Some Rules for Sanitation. Journal of the American Dietetic Association, Vol. 26, pp. 962-966. December, 1950.

Lieberman, James. Preventing Diseases Through Food Service Personnel Training. Journal of the American Dietetic Association, Vol. 29, pp. 248. March, 1953.

Fritz, John H. Sanitation in Food Service Department. Journal of the American Dietetic Association, Vol. 29, pp. 565. June, 1953.

Snyder, Walter F. Built in Sanitation. Journal of the American Dietetic Association. Vol. 31, pp. 119, Feb. 1955.

Chapter IX

MERCHANDISING

Good food, attractively displayed is the keynote of merchandising and salesmanship. The effort put forth to produce good food can be largely lost if good merchandising techniques are not used. A manager of a commercial food unit wants to sell the food that is prepared; a hospital dietitian wants her patients to eat the food needed and ordered by the doctor; and a school lunchroom manager wants to educate the children to select food that is good for them. In short, merchandising should tempt people to buy and eat more of the right foods.

Food service is big business and competition is as keen in this as in any other big business. Formerly people tended to accept what was served them but now with the newer knowledge of nutrition, the wide variety of foods available and the many and varied types of eating places, a manager really has to use ingenuity and all appropriate merchandising techniques in order to keep guests happy.

If the various techniques discussed in previous chapters are utilized, quality food will be produced, and the manager and the workers will have time to do those "extras" that are really the keys to food merchandising. The satisfaction that comes from the creative and aesthetic aspects of food service will be a real boost to the workers' morale and will create a happier working team. The worker should feel proud to sell or serve the food.

A good rule for evaluating your merchandising is to put yourself on the other side of the tray or cafeteria counter. Would you be tempted to buy what you see there? Does the food have eye appeal and whet the appetite? There is a definite relationship between the aesthetic and psychological aspect of food and the physiological utilization of foods in the body. Tempting the appetite by eye appeal will greatly affect the way in which the body desires, accepts and digests the food. The wise manager appeals to all five senses in her merchandising.

The title of a well known book, "Give the Lady What She Wants" indicates true merchandising. A good manager should know what the customers want and what price they can pay. To be able to do this, it is necessary to know something of the customers' background, habits, likes and dislikes and other factors that will assist in making suitable and attractive menus. A good manager also realizes that quality food is the best aspect of merchandising. One cannot cover up poor food with garnish, sauces or other devices. Merchandising depends on good judgment. Food must not only look good, but it must be good, if customers are to be attracted and satisfied.

Assuming that the menus have been carefully made and that the production of food is of the best, the following points will help merchandise the food. The student of food service can suggest many others.

A. Follow Art Principles of Color and Design.
   1. Use colors that are complimentary or contrasting. Natural food colors will be more acceptable than will highly decorated or garnished food.
   2. Design the arrangement of every plate. It should be and can be a picture.
   3. Take care not to have the plates look too standardized in shape and design.

B. Appeal to Various Senses.
   1. Contrast or blend flavors skillfully. Preserve the natural food flavor. Flavor piques the appetite.
   2. Appeal to sense of smell with aromatic spices and herbs. The senses of smell and taste are closely allied.
   3. Contrast texture. The way the food feels both as to texture and temperature will affect the taste buds and influence the acceptability of the food.
   4. Merchandise food by providing quietness, dignity and beauty of atmosphere and appointments.

C. Display and Serve Foods Attractively.
   1. Use unusual, interesting but suitable dishes for service on counters or trays.

      Example:
      Soup served piping hot in an individual soup tureen will tempt a patient's appetite.
   2. Use interesting plate combinations employing contrast of color, texture and flavor.

D. Style Foods and Service.
   1. Use the element of surprise. Do something that differs from what your competitors do.
   2. Be venturesome. Try new and different foods as they come in the markets and do interesting things with them.
   3. Keep abreast with the changes in eating habits. Watch for fashion trends in food.
   4. Style method of serving.
      Example:
      Serving from a cart or buffet.
   5. Style menus. Menus may feature holidays, children's menus, seasonal or local foods, traditions or food customs.

E. Build up a "Specialty".
   1. Aim to have your food "talked about" because of its quality and unusual features.
   2. Feature at least one item that you do better than your competitors --your guests or patients will have a happy smile when they see it on the menu or tray.

F. Use Artistic and Appropriate Displays.
   1. Use bulletin boards for unusual, interesting or educational displays.

      Example:
      Nutrition charts
   2. Use interesting and artistic fruit or vegetable arrangements.
   3. Feature interesting china or glassware.

G. Be Aware of Sales Value of Well Groomed Personnel.
   These workers represent the management to the public and can reflect good relationship between staff, employees and guests.
   1. Select attractive and courteous waitresses, servers or tray maids.
   2. Instruct workers on necessary personal hygiene, good grooming, and good manners.
   3. Provide and maintain attractive, suitable and immaculately clean uniforms for workers.

Problems on Merchandising

1. Outline and carry out a study of your clientele.

2. Make a study of the popularity of food items; the effect of one food on the saleability of another; or other factors influencing popularity. Explain results.

3. Change counter arrangements, dishes or shapes of food to see effect on saleability.

4. Make a study of menu terminology and the effect on saleability.

5. Study effect on sales of suggested menus or tray displays.

6. Collect some interesting pictures of good merchandising.

BIBLIOGRAPHY

Dahl, J. O. Restaurant Management. New York: Harper Brothers.

Hoke, Ann. Restaurant Menu Planning. New York: Harper Brothers.

West, Bessie Brooks and LeVelle Wood. Food Service in Institutions. New York: John Wiley and Sons.

Bryan, Mary de Garmo. The School Cafeteria. New York: F. S. Crofts and Company.

Spearman, Rose. Merchandising Good Food at Reasonable Price. Journal of the American Dietetic Association, Vol. 14, pp. 117. February, 1938.

Watts, Betty M. Flavor in Foods. Journal of Home Economics, Vol. 31, pp. 673. December, 1939

Sweeny, May. Changing Food Habits. Journal of Home Economics, Vol. 34, pp. 457. September, 1942.

Dorcus, Roy. Food Habits - Their Origin and Control. Journal of the American Dietetic Association, Vol. 18, pp. 738. November, 1942.

Eppright, Ercel. Factors Influencing Food Acceptance. Journal of the American Dietetic Association, Vol. 23, pp. 579. July, 1947.

Easton, Alice. Five Factors that Affect Appetite Appeal. Restaurant Management. Pp. 840. June, 1948.

Barber, Edith. Development of the American Food Pattern. Journal of the American Dietetic Association, Vol. 24, pp. 586. July, 1948.

Callahan, Genevieve. Flavor and Flair. Journal of the American Dietetic Association. Vol. 30, pp. 259, March 1954.

Buik, Helen A. Making Food Worth Talking About. Journal of the American Dietetic Association. Vol. 33, pp. 132, Feb. 1957.

A Symposium: Color in Food. National Academy of Sciences and National Research Council.

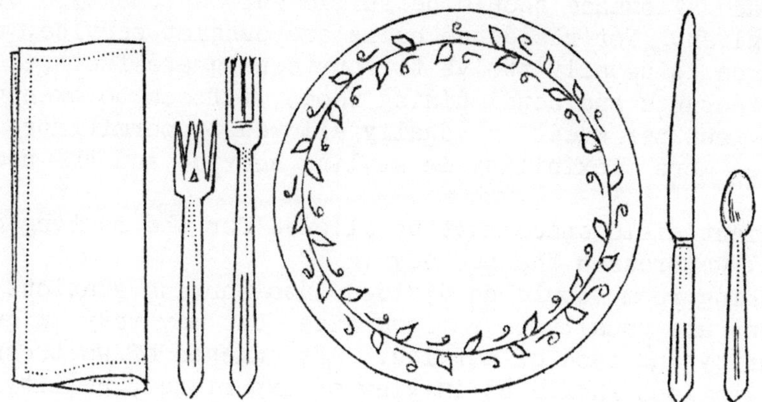

Chapter X

SERVICE OF FOOD

The dining room is the only part of a food establishment seen by the guest. It is, therefore, important that food be served with finesse and efficiency and that the waitresses be carefully selected and trained to give prompt, gracious and efficient service, for they represent the management to the guest. The food service unit which consists of the dining room, serving room and dishwashing unit is usually under the direction of a food service supervisor who is responsible for the coordinating of these units during the entire service period.

In order to accomplish this, there should be established for each unit:

1. Physical standards that make it possible to cut to a minimum the time between the finished preparation and the actual serving of food to the guest.

2. Personnel standards that will assure well selected, trained and competent personnel in each unit.

THE DINING ROOM

A. Physical Standards

1. The dining room should always be well ventilated, either by natural ventilation or by air conditioning. A constant temperature of 68° F. will insure the comfort of the guests.
2. Lighting should be adequate for efficient performance of the waitresses and for the comfort of the guest. It should also be attractive, soft and flattering.
3. Noise should be reduced to a minimum by use of resilient flooring and sound deadening material on walls and ceilings. Waitresses should wear rubber heels. The use of composition trays will also reduce noise.
4. Sanitation and cleanliness should always be keynoted. All floors, walls and tables should be easily cleaned. Daily dusting of all surfaces is essential.

5. The space allowance should be sufficient for the type of service to be given. For residence halls and banquet service, the space allowance is usually twelve to fourteen square feet per guest. In restaurants and hotel dining rooms, fifteen to twenty five square feet per guest is usually allowed to permit more individual service, more flexibility in styling service and the use of service tables.
6. Sufficient aisle space must be allowed for the routing of the guests, waitresses the bus boys.
7. The dining room should be divided into working stations. These stations are usually of uniform size, but may vary in guest popularity and ease of service. Assignments of waitresses to these stations should be in view of experience, ability, and efficiency.
8. Small tables of six to eight are preferable to long tables. This permits a quiet and more sociable atmosphere and makes service and routing easier.
9. The decoration should be simple and appropriate and should in no way interfere with the comfort of guests. Flowers should be artistically arranged and centerpieces should be below the eye level. Candles should be tall enough so that the flame is above the eye level.
10. All appointments including glass, silver, linen, china should be attractive and sparkling. The menu cards should be artistic.

B. Personnel Standards

1. Waitresses
   There should be a sufficient number of well selected and well trained waitresses for the plan of service to be used. Usually one waitresses for every eight to ten guests with an additional one for every twenty guests is allowed. The waitresses should be:
   a. Attractive and well-groomed. This includes careful personal hygiene to avoid body odors, clean fingernails, neatly combed hair in a hair net and no obvious make-up.
   b. Dressed in appropriate uniforms. This uniform consists of clean, well pressed dresses, hose, comfortable clean shoes, suitable foundation garment and slips of proper length with straps fastened, and no jewelry.
   c. Friendly, gracious and professional in attitude. There should be no unnecessary conversation with guests or fellow workers. They should stand erect when not serving and there should be no gum chewing in the dining room.
2. Waiters and Bus Boys should:
   a. Maintain the same standards for grooming and conduct as the waitresses.
   b. Wear suitable uniforms.

THE SERVICE AND DISHWASHING ROOMS

A. Physical Standards

1. An efficient service room adjacent to the dining room should be provided. There should be an exact plan for the placing of all foods, dishes, trays and silver.

2. The sequence of operations and the routing of all supplies should be planned. A chart showing this routing will be helpful. The serving room should be in complete readiness when the food arrives.
3. Sufficient and well planned equipment should be available. This consists of:
    a. Facilities for holding foods at the correct temperature-hot foods hot and cold foods cold-for the scheduled service time. This may involve the use of steam tables, heated carts, plate warmers, coffee urns, grills, refrigerators, banquet top tables and banquet rings. If the serving room is remote from the kitchen, double speed elevators or dumb waiters should be provided.
    b. Suitable small equipment for the service of all food.
    c. Sufficient number and correct size of trays for service.
    d. Duplicate service stations if large numbers are to be served.
4. The dishwashing area should be adequate, suitably placed, well equipped and efficiently arranged. There should be a careful plan for the return of soiled dishes so there is a minimum of confusion and noise.

B. Personnel Standards
1. There should be a sufficient number of well trained servers available.
2. The servers should be given definite assignments and instructions for their serving stations.
3. The servers should be instructed to serve with speed, neatness and efficiency.
4. There should be a plan for the inspection of all plates before they go into dining room.
5. Dishwashers should be given exact assignments and instructions in order to complete work quietly and efficiently.
6. All waitresses, waiters or bus boys should be given instructions on exact routing in obtaining food and in return of soiled dishes.

SERVICE IN DINING ROOM

Food served to groups may be served in many different ways depending on the functions, facilities and styling of the menu. Most types of table service for large groups are a modification of the English, Russian or Compromise service used in homes.

The Russian service implies formality. All the work is done by attendants from the side. Usually one waiter is allowed for six places. All food is passed from the side and the guests are either served by the waiter or they may serve themselves. This service is usually used in hotels.

The English service implies hospitality and informality with personal attention by the host or hostess. Everything is served at the table. This service, with some modification, is used in dormitories and residence halls where an upperclassman may act as hostess and serve all the food. In some cases they may only serve the meat, and the vegetables will be passed by the waiters. The desserts and beverages are usually served by waiters. Waiters usually serve ten to twelve covers.

The Compromise service implies plate service. It is quite distinctly an American modification and is used for large groups and for banquets. In this service, everything comes in from the serving room in individual service and is placed before the guest. There may be some modification of this to give more style and finesse to the service. For instance, the rolls may be passed from the side or the salad may be served in salad bowls. In some cases, vegetable plates or a dessert mold may be passed. The beverages may be poured at the table and cream and sugar passed.

Plate service is quicker to serve in the dining room but unless there is an excellent system used in the serving room and excellent coordination between dining room, serving room and kitchen, it may result in slow and uneven service in the dining room. This is not due to inefficiency of the waitresses, but usually due to slow service of plates in the serving room. See directions for serving room.

Cafeteria or self service is a common form of service. Often a combination of table and cafeteria service is used as in the nurses dining room in hospitals and in residence halls. In this case, the tables will be set up and cold foods may be served. Only the hot foods will be picked up at the counter. This cuts the time of standing in line to a minimum and also makes prompt service possible.

Smorgasbord service is used by the Scandanavians and implies tables loaded with meats, fish, cheese, salads, pickles, etc. These dishes may provide the main meal or they may be used as appetizers only.

Buffet service implies that either hot or cold foods or both may be served from a buffet table. All courses may be served from the buffet. If this is done, several tables are usually planned for the different courses. Modification may be used. The first course, desserts, and beverages may be served by waitress and the guests go to the buffet for the main course. Any other course may be featured in this way.

The type of service decided upon will vary with the aim, size, location and budget of the institution in which the food service is located. Food establishments can be classified as follows:

1. Low Cost - Cafeterias, self service unit.
2. Moderate Cost - Clubs, residence halls, and resort hotels.
3. Luxury or Semi-Luxury - Restaurants, tearooms and hotels.

Cafeterias and Self Service Units

This type of service is usually provided where the saving of time and money for the guest is the object. Cafeterias or some modification of them usually meets this need. The standards for cafeteria service will not be discussed here. For detailed directions on cafeteria service, see appendix.

Clubs, Residence Halls, Resort Hotels.

In these types of instutions, the group to be served is usually in residence. The service should be simple, quiet, inconspicuous and efficient, but should provide a congenial, informal and homelike atmosphere. The menu is usually a non-selective one. All guests are usually seated at one time. Some basic suggestions for service of these groups follow:

1. Waitresses or waiters should be well selected, well trained in standards for simple table service and sanitary work habits.
2. All workers should be given careful training and supervision. This is especially true if student workers are used.
3. The tables in the dining room should seat not more than six or eight guests. This will create a more homelike atmosphere.
4. A waiter should not be required to serve too many tables. The number assigned to him will vary with the type of service. Two tables to a waiter is usually the standard for good service.
5. The type of service used may vary as follows:
   a. All food served on plates in kitchen and brought to tables by waiters. Prompt and efficient service in kitchen and serving room is necessary. The waiter should bring all plates for one table at a time.
   b. All or part of the food may be served by the hostess at the table. This is called <u>hostess service</u>.

      <u>Example</u>:
      The meat may be served by the hostess and the vegetables passed by the waiter.
   c. Salads and desserts and beverages may be served individually by the waiter or may be served by the hostess at the table.

<u>Restaurants, Tearooms, Hotels</u>

The food service in these establishments assumes a more liberal budget, more leisurely dining, more formality and more individual service to each guest. The menu is usually a selective or à la carte menu. Some suggestions for this type of service follow:

1. Guests are seated at suitable size tables by the hostess and are given the menu.
2. Guests may write their order or the waitress may take the orders. They should be taken in sequence to avoid errors.
3. The waitress should be familiar with the items of the menu and any specific directions for styling of the service.
4. The waitress should be instructed in basic rules for table setting, service and removal of dishes.
5. The waitress presents the bill to guests on a tray and the guests may pay the cashier or the waitress may collect the money and return the change to guests.
6. The waitress should remove all dishes from tables and service tables as soon as guests leave.
7. The waitress may need to reset tables.

STYLING SERVICE

It is sometimes desirable to change the style of service for a special occasion or for better merchandising of food. Some suggestions for styling the various courses follow:

<u>Styling the First Course</u>

1. Juices, canapes or hors d'oeuvres may be served in the drawing room before guests come to dining room.

2. Appetizers served in the dining rooms, may be passed on trays or carts for guest selection. Suitable plates and silver should be placed before trays are passed.
3. Fruit or fish cocktails, sherbets or salad plates are usually placed after the guest is seated. The necessary silver is placed first. Accompaniments should be passed at once.
4. Soups may be served in soup plates, or individual soup tureens. They may be served from a large soup tureen in the dining room. Suitable spoons should be placed before placing the soup and any accompaniments passed at once.

Styling the Main Course

1. A hot plate may be placed before the guest and all food passed from side by the waiter.
2. The meat may be on the hot plate and vegetables passed, beautifully arranged on a vegetable plate.
3. Accompaniments to main course should be passed at once, usually by floaters.

   Examples:
   Roll baskets
   Relish plates

Styling the Salad Course

1. Individual salads may be placed between the removal of appetizer and service of the main course.
2. A salad bowl may be passed from which the guests will either serve themselves or be served by the waiter. The necessary plate and silver should be placed before passing the salad bowl.
3. A salad bar, tray or cart of assorted salads and assorted dressings may be used from which the guest may make a selection.
4. The salad may be served as a separate course either at the beginning of the meal or after the main course.

Styling the Dessert Course

1. Assorted desserts may be served from a dessert bar, cart or tray. A variety of sauces may be available.
2. Individual desserts may be placed before guests. Suitable silver should be placed before dessert is placed.
3. A large dessert mold or plate may be passed from which the guest may help himself or be served by waitress.
4. Special cakes, petit fours or cookies may be passed after desserts are passed.

Styling of Service by use of Buffet or Smorgasbord

This type of service may be used for one or several courses in a restaurant or tearoom. In order to have this service attractive and efficient, certain rules should be followed:

1. Provide equipment to keep hot foods hot and cold foods cold; such as chafing dishes, casseroles, grills, electric roasters, thermos jugs, iced bowls, pans or trays.

2. Arrange all foods served artistically. Feature unusual bowls, platters and trays. Use garnishes interesting in color and design.
3. Plan to keep foods replenished promptly so that the table always looks attractive. Food should never be held on the table too long.
4. Arrange tables so that the dining room is not too overcrowded to allow guests easy access to buffet tables.
5. Plan to seat guests and then invite them to the buffet in small groups, thus avoiding too long a line at buffet table.

SPECIFIC DIRECTIONS FOR TABLE SETTING AND SERVICE

After the general style has been determined, the waitress should be given specific instructions on the menu, the style of service, and the general routing of all activities. It is also necessary that each waitress be given instructions for table setting, service and clearing of tables.

Table Setting

1. Each waitress should be assigned specific tables and should be responsible for setting up, serving and clearing of these tables.
2. Each waitress should have access to a serving table on which can be placed water, extra silver or linen and a service cloth. Food, soiled dishes or linen should not be left on this table.
3. Waitresses should use the following procedures in setting tables:
   a. Set a cover for each guest; consisting of cloth or place mat, glass, napkin, china and silver consistent with the menu items and style of service.
   b. Handle all equipment in a sanitary manner.
      1) Silverware should be held by handles.
      2) Tumblers held by bases and goblets by their stems.
      3) Plates should be placed with the four fingers of the hand under the lower edge and the thumb on the upper edge of the plate.
   c. Use work simplification techniques to conserve time and energy.
      1) Use trays or carts to bring in silver, napkins, and other items required for the cover.
      2) Use trays to bring in all service equipment, water pitchers, ice bowls, tongs, etc.
      3) Do all of one phase of a job at one time, using both hands.

      Examples:
      Place silverware at all covers.
      Place all napkins.
      Place all the tumblers on the table at one time.

Table Service

1. Reduce all service to essential motions. Guests should never be conscious of service.
2. Load trays carefully to secure balance and to avoid slipping and spilling. Avoid overloading of trays.
3. Place and remove all food and dishes from left side of guest excepting beverage, which is placed at right. Use left hand for placing at left and right hand when placing at right.

4. Pass rolls, relishes or other serving plates to the left of guest and hold low enough so guests can serve themselves comfortably.
5. Refill water glasses and coffee cups from the right side. Never lift from table when refilling.
6. Handle all dishes correctly.
7. Use a small service tray when placing extra silver or replacing silver that has been dropped.
8. Place plates with monograms facing guest. Pie should be placed so that points face guests.
9. Use underliners for juice glasses, soup bowls, teapots or dessert dishes.
10. Serve beverages with the main course or dessert or both. Milk and tea are usually served with the main course and removed before serving desserts.
11. Coffee may be served with the main course and should be refilled for the dessert course.
    a. Milk should be poured into glasses from bottles in the dining room and placed at right of cover. When space allows an underliner should be used.
    b. Tea service should include a tea pot, hot water pot and an empty cup and saucer. The pots should be on underliners. The service is placed at the right of the cover.
    c. Coffee may be served in three ways:
        1) The filled cups may be brought from service area on a tray, placed on saucers at the service table and placed to right of cover.
        2) The empty cups may be brought in from service room and filled by waitress at service table.
        3) The empty cups and saucers may be placed on the table to right of the cover and the coffee poured at the table by the waitress.

<u>Clearing Tables</u>

1. Remove all service from the center of the table first: Salt and pepper shakers, condiment and relish plates, and other serving dishes. If they have been emptied earlier in the course, they may be removed at that time.
2. Remove all dishes from one place at a time.
3. Remove from left of guest using left hand to remove and the right hand to carry.

   <u>Example</u>:
   Remove main plate with the left hand, transfer to right hand. Remove salad and bread and butter plate with left hand and place on dinner plate behind the guest.
4. Remove any unused silver.
5. Refill water glasses and leave table until guest leaves.
6. Load trays of soiled dishes, glasses, and silverware, and carry them to the dish room.
    a. Stack platters, plates, and other heavy dishes in center of the tray. Plate waste may be removed to one of the plates or the tray.
    b. Separate the silverware and pile at one side of the tray.
    c. Place glasses on one section of the tray.

d. Place cups, milk bottles, bowls, cream pitchers and tea pots on one side of the tray.
e. Unload trays carefully in the dishwashing area as directed.

7. After guest leaves the dining room:
a. Collect and dispose of soiled linen as directed.
b. Wipe the table with a damp cloth and wipe chairs free from crumbs.
c. Return clean, usable food that remains in serving dishes such as relishes, condiments or rolls, to a designated location in the kitchen. Never save food that has been served to individual guests, though it may appear untouched.

SERVING THE BANQUET

Banquets are occasions when people of like interests gather together to enjoy sociability, good food and some type of entertainment. The surroundings should be attractive and suitably decorated to present a pleasant impression on the guests as they enter the dining room. The food must be good with no quality losses due to poor preparation or to too long holding. The service should be efficient and inconspicuous so as to interfere as little as possible with the guests and the program.

The planning and serving of banquets present many unique problems not found in other types of food service. For this reason, they will be discussed here in some detail. Detailed organization of all units with specific instructions for each unit and each worker is necessary if there is to be good coordination of kitchen, serving room and dining room.

<u>Some Essentials of a Good Banquet are</u>:

A. The Banquet Menu

The banquet menu should be simple, suitable for the occasion, well balanced nutritionally and it should be easily prepared and served by available workers. Special emphasis should be placed on flavor, texture, shape and color. The plates should be effectively garnished to stress color contrast and to add height to a flat looking plate. The menu should be "styled". This may be done by styling the food, the dishes used or the method of service.

<u>Example</u>:
Unusual relishes, assorted breads, colorful salads

Foods that can be counted or preportioned, will facilitate service by reducing the number of motions or operations in serving.

<u>Examples</u>:
Pork Chops vs. Roast Beef
Filet Mignon

Sufficient food should be provided for number expected, but some leeway must be allowed to meet emergencies.

B. The Dining Room

The dining room should evidence brilliance, due to cleanliness, smartness and simplicity. It should be formal, but exhibit friendliness and hospitality. The decorations should be suitable to the occasion. The appearance and attitude of the waitresses will help to carry out the desired effect. There should be a well planned seating arrangement, and the dining room should never be overcrowded. Tables of six to eight will be more pleasant for guests and are easier to serve as a unit. The long banquet type tables should be avoided when possible.

C. The Banquet Serving Room

The banquet serving room holds the key to a successful banquet. All dishes should be carefully planned and conveniently placed for service. The service room may be a permanent well equipped room or it may be a temporary one with make shift equipment. In either case, there should be facilities for keeping foods at proper temperatures during the service. A specific plan for service and routing is necessary and careful assignments should be given to all workers. Demonstrations will aid in the training program. The following equipment should be available for efficient service:

1. Duplicate serving centers to facilitate fast service.
2. Banquet top tables and banquet rings to make it possible to serve plates ahead. All waiters should get their plates at about the same time.
3. Large trays so that the waiters can carry in enough plates to serve all of one table at a time.
4. Dishwashing room which is well arranged and accessible to dining room, but so placed and constructed that the guests will not be disturbed during the program.

Instructions for Serving a Banquet

Banquet service must be prompt, quiet, inconspicuous and efficient. The general directions for service previously discussed apply, but the banquet service should be so planned that:

1. All guests in the dining room will be served the same course at about the same time (see serving room).
2. Everyone at a table should be served at one time so that guests will not have to wait for others near them to be served. The use of small tables will facilitate this.
3. Everything that goes with a course should be served promptly with that course: Rolls with main course; coffee, cream and sugar with dessert.
4. The guests at the speakers table should finish any course and the complete meal at about the same time as the rest of the guests so that the program will not be started too soon, causing confusion. It may be necessary to give this table a little slower service but it should be efficient.
5. The complete dining room should be cleared of a course at one time at the signal from the head waiter. All waitresses should have completed final service at the same time. All dishes, except water glasses should be removed from the tables and side tables so that there is no delay in the program.
6. All dishes should be handled quietly both in dining room and dish-washing room.

In order to serve a banquet successfully, careful plans of every detail must be made and all workers must be given specific table assignments, be informed of proper routing in the dining room and service room and in the proper grooming. All workers should wear suitable uniforms. A drill on techniques of table setting, serving and clearing is recommended.

The Banquet Personnel

1. Head waiter or waitress-who plans the service, trains all waitresses, bus boys and floaters; supervises table setting and coordinates all service and gives signal for clearing of tables.
2. Waitresses who are responsible for table setting, serving and clearing of the tables assigned. See directions for Table Service.
3. Bus boys who carry heavy trays from service room to waitresses' stations in the dining room. This speeds up service.
4. Floaters who may pass rolls, relishes, butter, fill glasses.

Coordination of the duties of these workers is essential for smooth and efficient service. While the bus boys are picking up plates from the serving room, the waitresses may be placing butter, salads, filling water glasses. It is not desirable to place butter and salads before the guests enter. Bus boys may supply certain stations or they may all go to farthest station first and then proceed to other stations. If bus boys are not used, waitresses may work in teams to better coordinate service.

PLANNING AND ORGANIZING A BANQUET

Careful planning and good organization of all details is essential to achieve a smoothly running and efficient function. Often inexperienced or volunteer groups are asked to serve a banquet. The work of the group may be divided into the following committees:

1. Planning
2. Production
   a. Range
   b. Salad
   c. Desserts
   d. Kitchen Clean-up
3. Serving room
4. Dining room

Each committee should be given definite instructions as to what they are to do and how to do it. A suggestion for assigning duties to each of these committees follows.

Planning Committee

1. Confer with group for whom the banquet is being given as to menu, seating arrangements, decorations and any other necessary instructions.
2. Decide on menu and recipes to be used.
3. Make market order, purchase and receive supplies.
4. Assign workers to the various committees.
5. Supervise during preparation and service.
6. Check and arrange for use of any leftovers after meal is over.
7. Make final statement as to cost.
8. Have a meeting of all committees to review function and make suggestions for improvement.

Production Committee

1. Analyze work to be done on each item on the menu.
2. Assign workers and make time schedule for all work to be done.
3. Prepare for service all items on menu as per directions.
4. Report leftovers to planning committee.
5. Clean up the kitchen.

Service Committee

1. Assign the work and post time schedules for workers.
2. Make a plan for the counter set-ups to be used. A posted chart showing this plan with assignment of workers will be helpful.
3. Make a requisition for:
   a. Any special serving equipment.
   b. All dishes, silver, glass and linen necessary to serve the menu.
   c. Arrange all equipment and dishes for service.
   d. Serve the food as it comes from kitchen. See discussion of Banquet Serving Room.
   e. Plan for clean-up of service room.
   f. Plan for dishwashing and storage of all dishes and equipment.
   g. Return any borrowed equipment.

Dining Room Committee

1. Make a chart of seating arrangement in the dining room.
2. Assign all workers to specific tables.
3. Plan decorations.
4. Give instructions to workers on:
   a. The menu.
   b. Table setting.
   c. Routing to service room and dishwashing area.
   d. Type and method of service.
   e. Clean-up dining room after function.
   f. Return any borrowed equipment.

Problems on Service

1. Plan, organize and serve a banquet for 200 people at a given cost.

2. Make a plan for various cost levels.

3. Make a plan for a variation of service.

4. Suggest standard forms to use in organizing a banquet.

BIBLIOGRAPHY

Service of Food

West, Bessie Brooks and LeVelle Wood. Food Service in Institutions. New York: John Wiley and Sons.

Fowler, Sina Faye and Bessie Brooks West. Food for Fifty. New York: John Wiley and Sons.

Lusby, Ruth. Training Restaurant Sales Personnel. U. S. Office of Education, Vocational Bulletin. No. 222, Washington, D. C.

Dunning, Frances, Standards for Cafeteria Service. Minneapolis, Minnesota. Burgess Publishing Company.

Bryan, Mary de Garmo, Alberta Macfarlane and E. R. Hawkins. Establishing and Operating a Restaurant. U. S. Industrial Series Bulletin. No. 39. Washington, D.C.

Chapter XI

PERSONNEL

No matter what standards may be set or what programs of control and performance may be initiated, the success or failure of the program depends finally upon the worker. If the worker knows the plan, understands what is to be accomplished and has a real desire to carry out this plan, his intelligent cooperation with adequate instruction and supervision will insure a satisfactory outcome.

It will not be possible to discuss here the overall personnel and supervision policies. An attempt will be made to touch upon a few points that will affect the performance of the worker who is responsible for food production and service.

The discussion will fall under the following headings:
- Description of the Job
- Selection of the Worker
- Training of the Worker
- Supervision and Follow Up of the Worker

Description of the Job

There should be a detailed word picture and analysis of all jobs to be done. This information is necessary to select intelligently the right type of worker, to standardize the number of workers necessary to do the job and to form a basis for training of the worker. There should be a definite ratio between wages and output of work. This involves defining what is to be done, when it should be done, who should do it and how long it should take.

To make a job description correctly, data should be kept on the various jobs or combinations of jobs. The method, tools and materials should be analyzed to cut the length of the job or in some cases eliminate it.

Selection of Worker

A worker will do best what he can do well. There are certain mental and physical qualifications that will make for a better grade of work and for a happier worker. Various interviews, written tests, and aptitude tests can be employed to ascertain the potential ability of a new worker. Education and past experience may also be a decided asset in many cases. In other cases, it is more desirable to take an untrained worker and give him the necessary training for the specific job.

The selection of the worker depends on:

a. Knowing the job with all its implications.
b. Knowing what qualifications of the worker will best fit him for the job.
c. Knowing sources of desirable employees.
d. Having the ability to estimate a worker's potential for a specific job.

Training the Worker

Too often a worker is given a new job with no specific instruction except what he can pick up from an older employee. He may learn some good points, but also some poor ones.

Any training program should involve:

a. Orientation of workers.
b. Planning the training of the worker in techniques, methods and in sequence of operations.
c. The selection of the best teaching techniques to accomplish the training.

Orientation of Worker

a. He should be introduced to his job.
b. He should be given an idea of the aim of the entire enterprise.
c. He should be made to feel the importance of his job and of each individual task in relation to the overall success of the operation.
d. He should be given an understanding of the personal hygiene and habits requisite to the job.

Training of Worker in Techniques and Methods

a. Decide who needs the training and in what.
b. Decide what common learnings could be given to groups or whether the instruction should be individual.
c. Make use of the job breakdown.
   1) Descripton of job
   2) Equipment to be used
   3) Sequence of operations, and whether continuous or occasional
   4) Key points to emphasize
   5) Necessary precautions
   6) Dangers

(See Clawson: Equipment Maintainence Manual)

Selection of Teaching Devices

a. Mimeographed or written material
b. Movies, explained and discussed
c. Practice, with encouragement

d. Supervision until new habit is formed and progress assured.

Often a combination of several devices can be most effective.

Example:
Teaching use of Mixer
   Give written instructions for use of mixer
   Show a movie of the correct use of mixer
   Demonstrate the correct use
   Have a worker demonstrate
   Have worker practice under supervision

Supervision of Worker

After any training program, whether it be formal or on-the-job training, there should be a follow-up until the supervisor is assured that the worker has formed a new habit and that he will not revert to the old habit.

Many failures in food production can be attributed to incorrect or inadequate information and instructions. The failures come when the worker is not guided and helped to carry out these instructions. Supervision is also necessary to help people work together to accomplish the total aim.

Supervision involves:

a. Knowing the various jobs, how and when they should be done and by whom.
b. Establishing good morale and communications with workers so that they will discuss problems as they arise, thus preventing failures.
c. Making certain all suitable equipment is in good working order and all material is available when needed.
d. Knowing the ability of the worker, his strong and weak points so that failures can be prevented.
e. Being able through scientific and technical knowledge to solve problems.

Suggested Problems in Training

1. Suggest some common techniques and learnings you would need to teach to all employees.

2. Suggest a training program or demonstration on some specific techniques to be used on a given job.

Suggested Problems on Supervision

1. List possible points of failure in making a cake and frosting, where adequate supervision might prevent failures. Carry on with other operations.

2. Supervise some specific unit during its operation.

BIBLIOGRAPHY

Personnel

Clawson, Augusta. Equipment Maintenance Manual. New York: Ahrens Publishing Company, Inc.

Lusby, Ruth M. Training Sales Personnel. Education Bulletin, Superintendent of Documents, Washington, D.C.

American Dietetic Association. A Guide to the Selection and Training of Food Service Employees. Minneapolis: Burgess Publishing Company.

Bryan, Mary de Garmo. The School Cafeteria. New York: F. S. Crofts and Company, Inc.

West, Bessie Brooks and LeVelle Wood. Food Service in Institutions. New York: John Wiley and Sons, Inc.

MacFarland, Alberta, and Mary de Garmo Bryan and E. R. Hawkins. Establishing and Operating a Restaurant. U.S. Department of Commerce. Washington, D.C.

Cooper, Alfred M. How to Supervise People. New York and London: McGraw-Hill Book Company.

Halsey, George D. Supervising People. New York and London: Harper Brothers.

Marstan, Kathryn. Cafeteria Supervision. Haviland Road, Stamford, Connecticut: Dahl Publishing Company.

Schmid, Merle D. Work Simplification in Hospitals. Industrial Management Engineers, 111 West Jackson Blvd., Chicago 4, Illinois. August 1947.

Whyte, William Foote. Human Relations in the Restaurant Industry. New York: McGraw-Hill Book Company.

Harrington, Mary M. Labor Practices in Hospital Food Service. Journal of the American Dietetic Association, Vol. 21, pp. 228. April, 1945.

Clawson, Augusta. Can Training Pay Dividends? Journal of the American Dietetic Association, Vol. 23, pp. 427. May, 1947.

Coffman, Ray. Developing Leadership in the Dietary Department. Journal of the American Dietetic Association, Vol. 25, pp. 126. January, 1949.

Childress, Clara. Training of Supervisors. Journal of the American Dietetic Association, Vol. 25, pp. 606. July, 1949.

Cohen, Irwin. The Supervisor, Past, Present and Future. Journal of the American Dietetic Association, Vol. 26, pp. 260. April, 1950.

Bonnell, Mildred. What Makes a Good Supervisor. Journal of the American Dietetic Association, Vol. 27, pp. 662. August, 1951.

Clawson, Augusta. A road Map for Training. Journal of the American Dietetic Association, Vol. 27, pp. 666. August, 1951.

Harrington, Mary M. A Dietary Aide Program. Journal of the American Dietetic Association, Vol. 27, pp. 636. August, 1951.

Hughes, R. Alberta. The Profession Studies Delegation of Duties. Journal of the American Dietetic Association, Vol. 27, pp. 634. August, 1951.

Prall, Charles, et al. Need for Training Auxiliary Workers. Journal of the American Dietetic Association, Vol. 27, pp. 638. August, 1951.

Roser, Foster B. Practical Personnel Management. Journal of the American Dietetic Association, Vol. 28, pp. 35. January, 1952.

Hughes, R. Alberta. What Do Ye More Than Others? Journal of the American Dietetic Association, Vol. 28, pp. 336. April, 1952.

Christenson, W. C. Supervisory Training. Journal of the American Dietetic Association, Vol. 29, pp. 569. June, 1953

Atkinson, Alta B. Development of Administrative Abilities. Journal of the American Dietetic Association, Vol. 29, pp. 144. February, 1953.

Miller, Gertrude E. and D. W. Weeks. Presupervisory Training-A Technique. Journal of the American Dietetic Association, Vol. 29, pp. 142. February, 1953.

APPENDIX

SUGGESTIONS FOR QUANTITY COOKERY LABORATORY

Aims of Quantity Cookery Courses May Be:

1. To gain, verify and apply knowledge of the scientific, economic and artistic aspects of producing quality food in quantity.

2. To develop in the student who is to become a future manager:
   a. Executive ability
   b. Reliability, judgment and independent thinking.
   c. Personality and professional attitude.
   d. Skill, efficiency and neatness in techniques.
   e. Knowledge of the organization and operation of a modern and efficient food service unit.
   f. High standards of food preparation and service.
   g. A good food sense

QUANTITY COOKERY LABORATORY

Facilities for teaching quantity cookery should be in a planned teaching laboratory where experiences of educational value can be afforded the students and where conditions can be controlled to make the best use of a student's time. This educational approach is difficult to maintain if a "service unit" is the only laboratory available. In a beginning class, the students learn to apply their theoretical knowledge to new situations; to use large equipment and processes; and to master some of the managerial aspects of quantity food service. When the laboratory experience is in a large service unit, the students often fail to see the entire picture of the operations and to correlate the various experiences. As an outlet for food production in quantity cookery classes, a cafeteria or student tearoom provides a splendid opportunity for students to see and integrate their many experiences. It is desirable that students have experience in both production and service so that they can complete studies started in the laboratory and can become acquainted with the public's food habits and their reactions to food.

LABORATORY PROCEDURES

Students should:

1. Use their scientific knowledge and training, and to this add shortcuts, methods and techniques applicable to quantity cookery.
2. Organize their work by making a plan and time schedule for all operations.
3. Be responsible for the finished products of the work assigned.
4. Taste and judge products critically.
5. Be conscious of the complete menu and overall operations in the kitchen.
6. Be responsible for keeping working space in order, wiping up anything that is spilled and washing and replacing all small equipment.

7. Be responsible for learning the use and care of all equipment and machinery used in each unit and know the cleaning techniques and sanitary standards.
8. Obtain all prices and data for assigned studies.

Serving Procedures

Students should be given experience in serving at the counter or in dining room so that they may have the opportunity to meet the public; to understand the problems of merchandising of food; and to complete the studies initiated in the laboratory.

Work Habits in Laboratory

1. Have all necessary material at hand.
   Examples:
   Recipe file
   Pads, pencils
2. Report in uniform
   White dress
   Hair nets
   Comfortable shoes
   Hose
3. Be well groomed
   Hair well combed
   No obvious make-up
   No body odors
4. Develop neat work habits
   a. Keep uniforms clean while working.
      Avoid:
      1) Wiping hands on uniform
      2) Leaning against tables or stoves
      3) Spilling or splashing
   b. Never touch face and hair while working.
   c. Wash hands after use of handkerchief.
   d. Use a tasting spoon for all tasting-never use fingers.
   e. Wipe hands on paper towels-not dish towels.

Suggested Plan for Laboratory Assignments.

The work performed during the laboratory period may fall into the following units or duties, and each student may rotate on these duties as assigned.

1. Range Unit
   a. Soups, meats, entrees
   b. Vegetable preparation

2. Bake Shop Unit
   a. Cake, puddings
   b. Pies, hot breads

3. Salad Unit
   a. Salad preparation and assembly
   b. Service room

4. Management
    a. Menus, requisitions and work sheets
    b. Special field trips
    c. Special problems
    d. Catering for special occasions

Suggestions for Student Assignments

Range Duty:

1. Prepare soup, entrees, and meat dishes.
2. Secure necessary instructions from cooks but work independently.
3. Learn yields, costs and special techniques for all dishes prepared.
4. Be alert to organization of the range unit as a whole, noting all food prepared and served from this unit.
5. Learn use and care of stoves, steamers, and all machines, attachments and small equipment used in this unit.
6. Learn the cleaning schedule for this unit.
7. Make special studies.
8. Serve meats at counter and carry through tabulation, shrinkage, cost, and other studies if assigned.

Suggested Studies

1. Using tabulation sheet, make a study of real vs. apparent cost of a meat.
2. Make shrinkage studies in relation to various cuts, grades or methods of preparations.
3. Determine the amount of meats to order for desired per capita yields.
4. Learn standard per capita servings for various kinds and cuts of meat.
5. Study utilization of leftovers from range unit.
6. Make time studies on various methods of preparation.
   Example: Hand vs. machine.
7. Compare quality of various methods of preparation.
   Example: (a) Steam cooking vs. range, (b) Variation of temperature.
8. Study literature for new meat and meat substitute dishes to add to menu chart.
9. Test or enlarge a new recipe for the range unit.

Vegetable Duty:

1. Prepare vegetables on this duty.
2. Get general instructions but work independently.
3. Learn yields, costs, and special techniques for dishes assigned.
4. Be alert to the unit as a whole.
5. Learn the use and care of all equipment used in the preparation and serving of vegetables.
6. Judge the quality of vegetables as purchased, noting waste in preparation.
7. Learn the yield of market units of vegetables.
8. Make time, cost, and yield studies on vegetable prepared.

9. Make studies on the effect of different methods of cooking on the quality of the finished product.
10. Carry out the staggered cooking of vegetables during the serving period.

Suggested Studies

1. Outline and carry out a study to determine the most economical size and shape of vegetable to be used in a potato peeler. Study time, waste and shrinkage.
2. Determine what vegetables are practical to peel by machine.
3. Outline a study on hand vs. machine-peeled potatoes. Give data.
4. Study tables for average per capita servings of vegetables. How can these be checked and standardized?
5. Make a comparative study of various methods of cooking vegetables. Example:
   Steam, surface or trunnion kettle cooking of vegetables.

Salad Duty:

1. Prepare salads:
   a. Prepare lettuce and other greens
   b. Prepare salad ingredients
   c. Assemble salads
   d. Make time, cost and yield studies in salads.
2. Make salad dressings.
3. Learn use and care of all equipment used.
4. Learn counter set-up in preparation for service.
5. Make coffee and learn the use and care of coffee urn.

Suggested Studies

1. List short cuts learned on this duty.
2. Make a time study for assembling 50 salads. Repeat, improving your speed.
3. Design a salad.
4. Review magazines or cookbooks for new ideas for salad or salad dressings.
5. Make a comparative study on various ways of making coffee.
6. Test coffee after holding for different lengths of time.

Bake Shop Duty:

1. Make pies, cakes, sauces, puddings and hot breads.
2. Review principles involved in products assigned.
3. Bring recipes adjusted as to amounts, of products assigned.
4. Make time and motion studies.
5. Learn use and care of all equipment used.
6. Note the work sheets, time schedules and general organization of the unit.
7. Judge the quality of the finished product.
8. Make cost and yield studies.
9. Carry out the staggered baking of the hot breads during service period.

Suggested Studies

1. Suggest variations of basic recipes.
2. Make a substitute study of some ingredient, judging the product for cost, yield and quality.
3. Compare yield and time on hand vs. machine mixed product.
4. Make shortcut studies.

Management Duty:

On this duty the student may follow this suggested sequence:

1. Complete menu chart.
2. Study and evaluate available quantity cookbooks.
3. Study menu pattern of unit.
4. Make menus for three or more days. Have these checked for balance, interest and suitability.
5. Make one or more days menu to be used.
   a. Make requisition
   b. Purchase foods
   c. Make a work sheet
   d. Pull recipes
   e. Check supplies as they come in.
   f. Supervise the production and serving of menu.
   g. Make out food consumption sheet at end of meal.
   h. Evaluate the problem

Suggested Studies

1. What foods sell best on counter?
2. How fast does line move?
3. How can you speed up line or service?
4. What is the average check?
5. Make a tabulation study and interpret results.

SUGGESTIONS FOR CAFETERIA SERVICE

1. Everything should be in readiness for service before guests enter.
   a. All heated units heated.
   b. All serving equipment available.
   c. All food suitably supplied.

2. Servers should be instructed in:
   a. Menu items
   b. Prices of menu items
   c. General ingredients of dishes
   d. Proper serving dishes
   e. Proper portioning

3. Servers should:
   a. Maintain good posture and be at attention at all times.
   b. Servers should be courteous to guests. "The guest is always right". Avoid visiting with friends or employees while serving.
   c. Be alert and constantly watch people in line to anticipate their wants.
   d. Develop skill and rapid technique in serving. Avoid waste motions. Serve portions with one motion rather than several.
   e. Not leave serving station without reporting to supervisor.

Service at Steam Table

1. Keep line moving. Each person at the counter is responsible for moving the line along. Help patrons make a choice by tactfully suggesting an item.

2. Maintain attractive appearance of steam table and insets.
   a. Exchange full pans for empty ones. Do not put fresh food in soiled pans.
   b. Serve food from back of pan toward front in an orderly system across the pan.
   c. Dip from bottom of a deep inset:
      Example:
      Soup-to get maximum heat.
   d. Wipe up any food spilled with damp cloth.
   e. Notify runner when menu items are low, but before exhausted. Notify supervisor if menu items are no longer available.

3. Serve plates neatly and attractively.
   a. Serve food on properly heated or chilled plates.
   b. Place foods within rim of plate.
   c. If accidents occur in serving, send back the plate to the kitchen or wipe off anything spilled with clean cloth. Never put food on plates and take it off again. Take a clean plate if customer desires to change his order.
   d. If double order is desired, place the two orders on opposite sides of the plate to facilitate checking.

Service at Salad Counter

1. Be familiar with salad ingredients and dressings.

2. Arrange artistically on counter with contrast of colors.

3. Arrange salads attractively in uniform rows both vertically and horizontally and move them forward from the back rows to the front as they are removed by the customers. This insures their being taken in rotation. Keep rows straight when replacing salads on counter.

4. Place salads so that the highest part of the lettuce cup is at the back of the plate in order that the customer may see the salad.

5. Watch reserve supplies and notify supervisor when supply is running low.

Service at Dessert Counter

1. Plan for an attractive and orderly arrangement of desserts. Plan contrasting colors and shapes.
   a. Place desserts in straight rows.
   b. Arrange pieces of pie with points toward customer.
   c. Center pie and cake on plates.
   d. Place cakes in same position on plates so icing side is visible to the customer.

2. Keep counter clean, wipe up anything spilled.

3. Keep dishes moved forward on the counter from back to front so that no dessert will stand on counter for a long period.

4. Watch reserve supplies and notify supervisor if menu items are not available.

Service at Beverage Counter

1. Check counter to be sure everything is in place before serving period begins. Maintain this status throughout the service period.

2. Serve beverages in hot cups.

3. Watch approaching customer and ask whether he desires coffee or tea. Never serve hot beverages until ordered.

4. Fill a cup to 1/2" of top before placing it on a clean saucer.

5. When serving tea, fill pot with boiling water to within one inch of top to avoid spilling from spout.

6. Notify supervisor if supplies are running low.

SPECIAL PROBLEMS AND TERM PAPERS

Each student may carry out a special problem or term paper which will require readings, conferences, laboratory experimental work and a written report. These reports may be given in class.

Each student should make an appointment for a conference soon after the assignment is given. If a student requires special testing material, a requisition should be in at least three days before use. Any special arrangements should be made with the instructor in advance of laboratory period. Suggestions for these studies appear at end of each chapter.

Form for Term Paper

General Form

Aim or Objective of Problem

Review of Literature

Laboratory Procedure

Steps and time schedule
Requisitions for supplies
Requisitions for special equipment
Technique
Special arrangement

Data and Observations

Results and Summary

Recommendations Applicable to Quantity Cookery

Bibliography